# Hiring
# Right

# Hiring
# Right

Conducting **Successful**
**Searches** in Higher Education

SANDRA **HOCHEL**
CHARMAINE E. **WILSON**

JOSSEY-BASS
A Wiley Imprint
www.josseybass.com

Published by Jossey-Bass
A Wiley Imprint
989 Market Street, San Francisco, CA 94103–1741          www.josseybass.com

Limit of Liability/Disclaimer of Warranty: While the publisher and author have used their best efforts in preparing this book, they make no representations or warranties with respect to the accuracy or completeness of the contents of this book and specifically disclaim any implied warranties of merchantability or fitness for a particular purpose. No warranty may be created or extended by sales representatives or written sales materials. The advice and strategies contained herein may not be suitable for your situation. You should consult with a professional where appropriate. Neither the publisher nor author shall be liable for any loss of profit or any other commercial damages, including but not limited to special, incidental, consequential, or other damages.

Readers should be aware that Internet Web sites offered as citations and/or sources for further information may have changed or disappeared between the time this was written and when it is read.

Jossey-Bass books and products are available through most bookstores. To contact Jossey-Bass directly call our Customer Care Department within the U.S. at 800-956-7739, outside the U.S. at 317-572-3986, or fax 317-572-4002.

Jossey-Bass also publishes its books in a variety of electronic formats. Some content that appears in print may not be available in electronic books.

Library of Congress Cataloging-in-Publication Data

Hochel, Sandra.
    Hiring right : conducting successful searches in higher education / Sandra Hochel, Charmaine E. Wilson. — 1st ed.
        p. cm.
    Includes bibliographical references and index.
    ISBN 978-0-470-18087-7 (pbk.)
    1. Universities and colleges—Employees—Selection and appointment—United States. 2. College personnel management—United States. I. Wilson, Charmaine E. II. Title.
    LB2331.67.S44H63 2007
    378.1'1—dc22                                                        2007024500

Printed in the United States of America
FIRST EDITION
*HB Printing* 10 9 8 7 6 5 4 3 2 1

# Table of Contents

# About the Authors

*Sandra Hochel* is distinguished professor emerita of communications at the University of South Carolina Aiken. She has spent most of her 33-year career in higher education as a faculty member, teaching courses in intercultural, interpersonal, interviewing, public communication, and communicating in professional contexts. In addition she has served as department chair, director of an interdisciplinary studies program, head of a division of arts and letters, and chair of a faculty governance organization. She is a Fulbright Scholar who taught in a business communications program in Hungary, the recipient of several teaching and service awards, and a former lecturer for Semester at Sea. She has longstanding involvement and interest in employment selection, having served on 40 search committees (chairing 15 of them), including ones for chancellor, vice chancellor, system president, and other administrators and faculty. She has given numerous workshops and presentations on conducting effective searches for faculty and administrators. Her main areas of scholarship are in intercultural communication and communication education, which have involved sharing communication strategies and methodologies to help others improve their success in a variety of contexts. She received her bachelor's degree from the University of Texas at El Paso and her master's and doctorate degrees from Purdue University.

*Charmaine E. Wilson* is associate professor of communications at the University of South Carolina Aiken. At USCA, she teaches classes in interpersonal, group, and organizational communication as well as interviewing. Her interest in employee selection, organizational socialization, and institutional effectiveness has influenced much of her work at USCA. She was instrumental in improving the orientation programs for new students and in helping enhance the academic advisement of new students. In addition, she helps introduce new students and their parents to the culture of higher education. She has chaired or served on more than a dozen search committees at USCA and has assisted with many more by evaluating presentations, participating in role-plays, and conducting interviews. Prior to coming to USCA in 1991, she was a senior management consultant and trainer with MOHR Development (1990–1991) and London House (1989–1990) where she worked with a wide range of industry and nonprofit clients to enhance the selection, development, and retention of qualified employees. At London House, she worked to enhance the validity of the selection process by developing several structured interviews for both nonprofit and for-profit organizations. Dr. Wilson is the author of several publications including "Structured Interviewing: The Next Generation of Selection Systems" in the *Journal of Staffing and Recruitment.* She has given numerous presentations and workshops, several relating to the hiring process. She earned her bachelor's degree from the University of Montana, her master's degree from Purdue University, and her doctorate in organizational communication from the University of Washington.

# Foreword

What makes this book especially useful is its grounding in organizational communication theory and research. *Hiring Right* provides department chairs, faculty members, and administrators with theory-driven, yet hands-on information and advice for managing the very critical hiring process.

Of the many changes anticipated in higher education over the next decade is the retirement of the baby boom generation and the subsequent need to hire a number of new colleagues to replace those retirees. Hochel and Wilson's emphasis on communication provides readers with the essential tools to form search committees that work effectively, recruit strong applicant pools, evaluate candidate files, interview candidates to determine if they match preset criteria, identify top applicants, hire them, and do what needs to be done to ensure the new hire's successful transition to campus.

The authors also challenge search committees to hire candidates who are a good match by integrating communication theory and practice to help committees find candidates who will share institutional values, have longevity in the unit, and be good colleagues. The guidelines articulated in this book allow readers to uncover these important traits in job candidates.

Every search committee member, department chair, and campus administrator would be well served having this book as a reference. I wish this guide had been written much sooner, and am delighted that it is available now.

*Betsy Wackernagel Bach, Ph.D.*
Second Vice President, National Communication Association
Chair, Department of Communication Studies
University of Montana–Missoula

# Preface

This book is a practical guide for anyone involved with hiring in higher education. We've written it for busy faculty, staff, and administrators who want to conduct more efficient, fair, and effective searches, but who don't have time to investigate the large body of research on employment selection and communication or dig through multiple sources to uncover recommendations established and proven through the years. We've written this book for campus leaders, search committee chairs, and committee members who want to increase their ability to accurately predict a candidate's success at their institution.

The ideas and information in this book are an outgrowth of our intertwined experiences as communication faculty and search committee members. We have years of experience chairing and serving on search committees. We've been effective in our roles; in fact, we've been asked to lead high-profile searches and provide guidance to colleagues engaged in hiring. Our success has not been happenstance. It is a result of our expertise in communication combined with the ongoing process of learning from our successes and failures on searches. Effective communication is key to hiring right, from initial committee deliberations to extending the offer. Throughout the book, we apply our knowledge of interviewing, interpersonal processes, intercultural interactions, persuasion, and organizational and group communication and offer specific recommendations based on communication principles and relevant research.

## FEATURES OF THE BOOK

In this book we take you through the hiring process step by step. We cover topics ranging from deciding the size of the committee and who should serve to extending the offer and welcoming the new hire and all the topics you would expect in-between. Here are some highlights:

- Numerous sample documents (e.g., letters of acknowledgement and rejection, emails with candidates, forms for evaluating applicants' credentials and letters, forms for receiving feedback from those who interact with visiting candidates)
- Recommendations for analyzing a position, establishing job criteria, and wording the position announcement
- Concise discussion of Equal Employment Opportunity regulations with a focus on ways to ensure compliance
- Techniques for recruiting well-qualified and diverse candidates
- Procedures for systematically evaluating candidates throughout the process
- Techniques for interpreting information in vitae, applications, and reference letters
- Strategies for obtaining in-depth, honest evaluations from references
- Strategies for conducting effective phone and campus interviews with candidates
- Tips for writing interview questions and examples of questions that go beyond the obvious and expected
- Multiple methods for gathering information during campus visits
- Discussion of perceptual and cultural biases that can unfairly hurt candidates
- Tips for communicating effectively with candidates
- Recommendations for avoiding major mistakes throughout the process

## ACKNOWLEDGEMENTS

We are indebted to the many people who provided us with assistance during the development and writing of this book. Many colleagues at the University of South Carolina Aiken helped us formulate our ideas and clarify our thinking, and we appreciate their insights and support. We are particularly grateful to the manuscript reviewers who carefully read our work and provided constructive suggestions for improvement:

- Jeff Cargile, Director, Human Resource Programs and Services, University of South Carolina Columbia
- Maria Chandler, Director of Human Resources, University of South Carolina Aiken

- Tim Edgar, Associate Professor and Director of the Graduate Program in Health Communication, Department of Marketing Communication, Emerson College
- Jane Tuten, Director of the Library, University of South Carolina Aiken

Their thoughtful suggestions helped us improve the quality of this book. Carolyn Dumore at Anker Publishing also offered valuable assistance. We appreciate her efficiency and expertise, as well as her confidence in us. We thank Dr. Betsy Bach for graciously taking the time to read the manuscript and write the foreword. Finally, a personal word of thanks to our partners, Bob and T.J., who provided unfailing encouragement and sound advice throughout the process.

*Sandra Hochel*
*Charmaine E. Wilson*
University of South Carolina Aiken
February 2007

# Chapter One

# The Importance
# of Hiring Right

The ultimate success of any college or university depends on the quality of the people it hires. Hiring good people is axiomatic: No one questions its importance. Management consultant and former Stanford faculty member Jim Collins discovered how important hiring decisions are in the business world when he and his research staff spent five years investigating how some companies were able to move from good to great. When he began his research, he expected to discover that the most important characteristic of becoming a great company was establishing a vision and defining strategies for success. Instead he discovered the first and requisite characteristic of becoming great was hiring the right people for the right job (Collins, 2001). Although differences certainly exist between commercial companies and colleges and universities, we believe Collins's research on hiring applies to higher education. If you want your department or unit to achieve excellence, the most important thing you can do is to hire the right person for your position.

Everyone wants to hire right, but how do you do this? Unfortunately, there are no quick answers, no gimmicks, no 100% guarantees. But this doesn't mean you can't improve your chances of hiring the right person. Indeed, we have written this book because we believe you can significantly increase your chances by using proven strategies, being thorough and systematic, and applying the research on employment selection and communication. We've taken research-based guidelines and best practices and adapted them to higher education to help faculty, staff, and administrators conduct efficient, fair, defensible, and successful searches.

## THE IMPACT OF THE HIRING DECISION

We've all worked with good colleagues and with bad ones. We know well the joys and frustrations of both. Here are a few examples of problems that can result from a bad hire:

- A unit's reputation as a cohesive and capable department—developed over several years of good work—is seriously eroded in the eyes of the administration because of problems created by a series of poor hires.
- A newly hired department chair is inefficient and ineffective. Faculty are aggravated and discouraged. Some begin job hunting.
- The workload of a unit's staff is significantly increased because a new hire is not pulling her weight and spends a great deal of time complaining and spreading dissension. Stress is going up and morale is going down.
- A supervisor spends far too much of his time training, coaching, reprimanding, and documenting because a new hire's performance is seriously problematic. Others in the unit are getting frustrated and feel anger toward both the new hire and the supervisor.
- Admissions to the college are affected because the recently hired admissions director is not as competent as she appeared on paper and in the interview. Staff members are disgruntled, the work flow is in disarray, and several prospective students have been turned off by her brusque demeanor.

These examples deal primarily with the emotional, relational, and workload consequences of making a bad hire. But these are not the only problems that arise. Think about the cost of a mediocre hire. The hire may stay at your college for a lifetime doing only a marginal job, not poor enough to be fired, but not good enough to help the unit or institution achieve excellence. Think also about the consequences of a truly awful hire—the employee whose performance is poor enough to warrant firing. The time and energy for the termination process can be substantial. The impact on morale can also be significant. Some coworkers may be relieved but others may fear for their own jobs. The financial cost can also be substantial. HireSmart (2006), a consulting firm with more than 20 years of experience, estimates the cost of replacing a professional or managerial employee at about a year's salary and benefits. And that is

---

EXHIBIT 1.1

**Summary of the Consequences of a Bad Hire**

- Increased workload for other employees.
- Frustration and resentment resulting in low morale.
- Decline in unit effectiveness.
- Waning of unit reputation.
- Turnover of effective employees.
- Wasted dollars.

---

only the cost of replacement. If the termination is contested, the costs can be staggering.

Of course, when you hire the right person for your opening, you add quality to the unit and the institution. Good hires should improve the unit's effectiveness, increase retention, attract other good employees and students, and enhance the unit's reputation. And a good hire can create a positive ripple effect in a unit and institution, improving the quality of everyone's efforts.

## THE CHALLENGE FOR HIGHER EDUCATION

In spite of the importance of the hiring process, few of us in academia are trained in employment selection. One writer in *The Chronicle of Higher Education* considered it "shocking" that colleges and universities "spend so little time or money learning how" to conduct searches. He observed that in his 15 years in higher education, many spent in administration, he had received not "one hour of formal training in the best practices for hiring" (Dettmar, 2004, p. B6). In addition to a lack of training, most in academia must add the search responsibilities to their regular duties. So they have no released time to conduct the search or to learn about best hiring practices.

Because most persons involved in hiring aren't trained in best practices and are busy with their other duties, they sometimes engage in poor practices. For example, administrators or search committees may fail to conduct a position analysis and establish specific job qualifications, resulting in inaccurate selection criteria, or they may rely on limited recruitment avenues and attract only a weak pool of applicants. Committee members may not read between the lines on a curriculum vitae or in reference letters and thus obtain an inaccurate picture of a candidate. They may fail to follow the Equal Employment Opportunity laws and risk a lawsuit or may rely almost exclusively on the interview rather than use multiple methods of information gathering.

Not only are most in academia not trained in employment selection, most are also not trained in communication. From start to finish, the selection process is a communicative one requiring skills in persuasion, interviewing, and group and interpersonal communication. When people fail to realize the importance of communication in the process, they sometimes engage in poor practices. For example, those involved in a search may not write a persuasive ad that appeals to a diverse, well-qualified audience. They may skip the important step of preparing a set of well-written standardized questions to ask of all candidates and references or may use poor techniques when interviewing references and candidates, thus gathering incomplete or inaccurate information. Committee members may be unaware of cultural differences in persuasive styles and miss good candidates. They may not agree on rules for decision-making in the beginning of the process and set themselves up for contentious deliberations.

Lack of time and training is one impediment to hiring right—the attitudes of some are another. Not everyone is convinced that how a search is conducted increases the chances of hiring right. Some seem to believe the outcome is a matter of luck. We once heard a faculty member compare the selection process to a stab in the dark. In his experience, the process provided little valid information and frequently gave an inaccurate picture of how candidates would perform once on campus. Yet we know this faculty member spent little time checking references or verifying other information, and he treated the candidate interview as spontaneous conversation. It's no wonder the outcome was a matter of chance.

Our experience and knowledge of relevant research have taught us that actions affect outcomes. For example, research has repeatedly shown structured interviews have higher predictive validity than unstructured interviews (Schmidt & Hunter, 1998). By using structured interviews, then, you increase the chance of making an accurate prediction of the candidate's success. Similarly, we know from personal experiences that calling unlisted references (with the candidate's permission) and asking discerning questions yields valuable information that can also enhance predictive validity. When a search is viewed as a deliberate and systematic process of gathering and evaluating information and when proven strategies are followed, it is far from a stab in the dark.

## THE BENEFITS OF CONDUCTING A GOOD SEARCH

As we have discussed, following the guidelines for conducting an effective search improves your odds of making a good hire. But you can also reap other benefits. First, you can save time by learning from the experiences and knowledge of others and not reinventing the wheel. You can also save money and energy by preventing failed searches. In addition, the process can be smoother, less contentious, and thus more enjoyable. And perhaps more importantly, you can be confident that you have conducted a fair and defensible search.

Let's take an example. We recommend agreeing on performance criteria in the beginning of the process. When you agree in advance on the criteria, the final decision-making is less time consuming and potentially less argumentative. If you review each file using evaluation forms based on clearly defined performance criteria, you avoid going over a file multiple times and evaluate candidates more fairly. By using the evaluation forms we recommend, adhering to Equal Employment Opportunity regulations, and following our advice on note-taking, you have the documentation needed to defend your decision and write a convincing final report. You've saved time and energy, avoided unnecessary hostility, and conducted a search that is unbiased and sound.

Consider a second example. We offer several recommendations for recruiting well-qualified and diverse applicants. If you carefully word the ad and effectively disseminate the information, you can expect a larger, more diverse, and well-qualified pool of applicants. Obviously, this increases the chances of finding the right person, but it also helps prevent failed searches and saves the time, expense, and frustration of repeating the search. If you follow our suggestions for crafting the position announcement, you will have the information needed to fairly evaluate files in a timely fashion and keep the search on track. Similarly, our suggestions for communicating effectively with candidates should save you time by helping you to be clear and comprehensive. They can also help prevent failed searches by keeping applicants interested in your position. When you conduct a search well, the benefits are far-reaching.

## OVERVIEW

To help you enjoy the benefits of conducting a good search, we provide a practical orientation based on research and experience to guide you systematically through the hiring process from beginning to end. In Chapters 2 through 4, we offer guidance for laying the groundwork for an effective search. More specifically, in Chapter 2 we discuss the importance of selecting a good search committee, establishing operating procedures, and understanding and adhering to Equal Employment Opportunity guidelines. In Chapter 3, we cover the critical activities of defining the position duties and needed qualifications so you can determine your information needs and write a persuasive position announcement. Because you need to have a strong pool of applicants, we make recommendations for effective recruiting in Chapter 4.

The remaining four chapters focus on gathering and evaluating information to make defensible judgments about your candidates. In Chapter 5, we offer strategies for the systematic evaluation of the candidate-submitted materials as well as letters of recommendation. After careful evaluation of materials, you must identify the top candidates and gather additional information on them, especially through phone interviews and reference checking. We provide suggestions for how to be effective in these processes in Chapter 6. Chapter 7 is dedicated to the campus visit. We recommend using multiple methods of information gathering and present a variety of options. We also discuss strategies for making the campus visit a success. Finally, in Chapter 8, we discuss evaluating all the information gathered to make a final decision, paying particular attention to problematic pitfalls and biases. We conclude the book with recommendations for finishing the job search.

# Chapter Two

## Form and Charge the Committee

Suppose you decide to remodel your home. You would never think of hammering the first nail without considering your needs and wants, finding a builder, setting a budget, and so on. You know making hasty decisions and cutting corners could cause problems. Likewise, when undertaking a search, careful planning is crucial. You must determine who will be involved in the search and develop a plan of action. Before the committee even writes the ad, members need to establish their ground rules and understand the law. This will save time and avoid potential headaches later on.

### ESTABLISH THE SEARCH COMMITTEE

A critical first step in the process is for the hiring authority to put together a good search committee. To help create a positive committee experience, that authority should consider which constituent groups need to be represented, the size of the committee and who should chair it, and who should represent the various groups. University policy should be reviewed as well for any guidelines it may offer on committee composition.

#### Identify the Constituent Groups

First, determine which constituent groups are most affected by the hire and then decide which of these groups need to be represented on the search committee. Keep in mind that you can involve some of the constituent groups in the process in other ways than serving on the committee.

Who are the constituent groups, and should they be represented on the search committee?

- *The hiring unit.* Coworkers and subordinates will usually make up the majority of committee members. Sometimes a sensitive question is whether to have the supervisor of the new hire serve as a voting member on the committee. At times this makes sense, especially if the supervisor will work closely with the new hire and knows the job well. Other times, having a supervisor on the committee is problematic, particularly if this person is likely to dominate or if others tend to defer to him or her. In this case, the supervisor should not be on the committee.
- *Interfacing units.* We recommend including at least one "outside member" because today's employees do not work in a vacuum. Having representatives from interfacing units helps ensure a new hire's success because people are more accepting of decisions when they have representation on the committee. In addition, employees from outside the unit bring different perspectives and may raise issues unit members might not consider. One important interfacing unit is human resources (HR). At a minimum, an HR representative can offer crucial information on legal issues and campus policies.
- *Students.* We recommend including students on a search committee for those positions that address student life and services. For most other hires, we find it better to involve students in other ways, such as attending presentations or meeting with candidates and sharing perceptions with the search committee.
- *Alumni, advisory boards, or community members.* When the success of the new hire will be directly influenced by interactions with these groups, consider including a representative on the committee; otherwise, involve these groups in other ways. For example, if you are hiring a director of experiential education, you should consider having a local business person serve on the search committee. Likewise, if you need an area of expertise not available on campus (e.g., golf course management), you might involve a community member. In either case, though, make sure the outside member has demonstrated a long-term commitment to the institution and has the time and motivation to serve. We've unfortunately seen cases where external members were appointed, did not participate in the process, but then chose to vote. This created anger and resentment and undermined the work of the committee.

When feasible, select a committee member who is able to represent more than one group to help keep the size of the committee manageable. We had a good experience, for example, including on one search committee an alumna of our department who is also one of our admissions counselors.

## Determine the Size of the Committee

Now think about the optimal committee size. We all know the larger the committee gets, the more difficult it is to bring people together and ensure effective participation of all members. So how large should the committee be? J. Dan Rothwell (2004), an expert in group communication, suggests using the smallest number of people capable of getting the job done effectively. When in doubt, Rothwell recommends 7 to 10 members. We've served on committees that ranged in size from 4 to 24, and as the size increases, so does the complexity of planning and deliberating. We realize some committees, such as ones for dean searches, may have to be large so all constituent groups are represented, but as a general rule, avoid large committees.

## Select the Committee Chair

What should you look for in a committee chair? You might be tempted to pick someone based on the prestige of her or his position. If so, we urge you to reconsider and select solely on characteristics that will help ensure the success of the committee. Choose someone who:

- Is well respected and trusted on campus
- Is a competent communicator (e.g., runs meetings efficiently; moves discussion on as appropriate and allows more talk when needed; deals with awkward situations skillfully; communicates with people from different cultures successfully; handles difficult group members effectively)
- Has excellent organizational skills
- Works well with the administration and the HR office
- Has institutional knowledge to provide the committee with needed information and history
- Has time to devote to running the search

### Identify Members for the Committee

The reality is that we rarely have the luxury of handpicking every member of the search committee. But when you do have a choice about who serves, look for people who are:

- Competent communicators
- Able to devote the time and energy needed
- Conscientious
- Highly credible
- Objective and critical thinkers
- Trustworthy and able to maintain confidentiality
- Able to ask tough questions tactfully
- Willing to make difficult decisions

When selecting individuals for the committee, also consider the diversity of the committee. Are different ages represented? Different ethnicities? Different races? Both sexes? A range of perspectives? Include individuals who value diversity. These efforts will help to ensure that different viewpoints are represented and to convey to a candidate the institution's commitment to diversity.

## SET THE GROUND RULES

### Cover the Basics

*Clarify the authority of the committee.* Is the committee charged with recommending candidates to the administration or does it have the power to make the hiring decision? Are you to rank order acceptable candidates or provide an unranked list? Be sure members understand the committee's authority.

*Know your budgetary limitations.* How many finalists can you bring to campus? Who must approve all expenditures?

*Review legal guidelines and university hiring policies.* Have an HR or legal representative review all legal considerations and relevant university policies with the full committee. Stress the responsibility of all to observe Equal Employment Opportunity guidelines and review the consequences of any violations.

*Stress the importance of confidentiality of applicants.* The names of candidates should be confidential until the finalists are announced unless your institution or state has a policy mandating openness.

*Develop a realistic timetable.* This can be one of your most difficult tasks. Do all you can to begin the search and advertise as early as possible. (See Chapter 4 for more information.) When developing the timetable, we begin with a target completion date and work backwards. Be mindful of the difficulty of doing business during holidays. Further, if students and nine-month faculty are involved in the search, plan the campus visits when they will be on campus.

### Set Guidelines for Handling Applications and Inquiries

*Decide if you will consider incomplete applications.* Whatever you decide, you must treat all files equally. The decision not to review incomplete files is particularly important if you have a firm application deadline because you cannot go back and reconsider incomplete applications. If you go this route, consider giving applicants some latitude on letters of recommendation or other material beyond their control, but not on candidate-prepared material.

*Decide if a subcommittee should reject unqualified candidates.* Most search committees receive applications from candidates who do not have the minimum job requirements. One of us served on a search for a chief academic officer, and we received applications from first-year faculty and community members with no managerial experience. If you expect to attract scores of applications or if your HR office doesn't screen out unqualified applicants, consider having a subcommittee eliminate those who do not meet the basic requirements mandated in the ad. Keep in mind that the subcommittee is not to judge the quality of a file, only basic job requirements. Two to three members review each file; if they agree, the file is removed from consideration. If they disagree, the file is considered without prejudice.

*Agree to refer all inquiries to the chairperson.* Because responses to questions about the positions must be consistent, one person needs to handle them.

### Determine Procedures for Screening and Deliberating

*Include all committee members in the evaluation process.* Once applicants have been deemed qualified, all committee members should individually screen and evaluate files without consulting with others on the committee. This encourages full and shared participation in the search process.

Individual evaluation also helps ensure that all members are prepared to voice their opinions so a variety of perspectives is brought to the table and it is harder for some members to dominate or promote their own agendas.

*Stress confidentiality of deliberations.* All members must feel free to voice concerns and preferences for or against candidates.

*In the initial screening, place each applicant in one of three groups: yes, no, or maybe.* In these early stages we recommend using three broad categories instead of numerical rankings because you do not have enough information to make fine distinctions. Rankings are also cumbersome in the early stages.

*Determine a method for making decisions.* You may have assumed you would make decisions by majority vote, but since some authors recommend search committees make decisions by consensus, you should clarify this in the beginning. Our recommendation is to use the democratic method since we believe attempting to reach consensus gives too much weight to difficult and argumentative members (if you have any of these). On many committees, attempting to reach consensus is likely to cause more conflict and tension than using the democratic method. Building consensus is a daunting, time-consuming, stressful process that is well worth the effort when specific conditions apply (see Rothwell, 2004). However, our experience is that such conditions rarely apply to search committees. Use of the democratic method is fair, efficient, and generally accepted. Later, we give recommendations on how to efficiently select the candidates who proceed to the next stage. For now, just establish the method of decision-making.

*Treat internal candidates as you do all others.* Having internal candidates can be a blessing or a curse. If you have an excellent one with a proven record, then this enriches your pool of candidates. If you have a poor candidate, then this can make the rejection awkward. The key to handling internal candidates is to treat them as you do all others. Obviously they must be evaluated on the same basis as others and receive no preferential treatment. If internal candidates are weak, never give them a courtesy interview just because you think this will help them save face. If they are strong and become semi-finalists or finalists, then you must check references, interview them in exactly the same way as others, provide the same itinerary if they have a campus visit, and so on. This is imperative for legal and ethical reasons.

## Establish Tracking Procedures

To help ensure that the search process goes smoothly, procedures are necessary to track information and progress on the search. These procedures are usually most helpful for the committee chair and any support staff working with the chair on the search, but can be useful for all members of the committees. Procedures need to be in place to keep track of all applicants, the materials they've submitted, and your communications with them. Contact your HR office to determine if online tracking is available. If not, develop a simple spreadsheet (see Appendix A). Further, if you do not review files electronically, we recommend having a form for the front of each candidate's file with a checklist of items to show the completeness of the file (see Appendix A).

## KNOW THE LAW

### Follow Equal Employment Opportunity Regulations

In 1964 the Civil Rights Act made it illegal to discriminate in employment on the basis of race, color, religion, sex, or national origin. The act also established the Equal Employment Opportunity Commission (EEOC) to enforce the law. Later the EEOC established uniform pre-employment regulations to assure that applicants from protected classes were not intentionally discriminated against because of their demographic group. A protected group is one the federal government has identified as needing special protection due to past economic discrimination or special status.

Since 1964, additional EEO laws have been enacted, including the Americans with Disabilities Act and the Age Discrimination in Employment Act. Current EEO laws make it illegal to discriminate on the basis of "race, color, ethnic identification, national origin, religion, sex, age, disability, and veteran status" (Weiss, 2004, p. 15). Some state laws add other protected classifications such as marital status, parenthood, and sexual orientation. (See Exhibit 2.1 for guidance on permissible and impermissible areas of inquiry.) All EEO regulations mandate that candidates be evaluated only on bona fide occupational qualifications (BFOQs), and that characteristics unrelated to the job not be considered.

In a few situations, one of the protected classifications may be a valid job requirement if the committee can provide compelling justification and if the HR office or legal counsel approves the justification. For example, some disabilities may keep an applicant from fulfilling an essential job function. In other instances, a religious institution may consider an applicant's religion. The key is whether the committee has established essential and defensible job requirements as explained in Chapter 3.

Unfortunately, too many people view EEO regulations as burdensome restrictions they are forced to follow to avoid lawsuits. However, we do not view these provisions as burdens but as benefits because they require committees to do what is right: to establish essential job requirements and then base decisions only on those requirements. By focusing search committees on job requirements, the regulations provide de facto protection for others. For example, a committee that might unfairly eliminate a candidate on the basis of political affiliation, hair length, or attractiveness is less likely to do so if members keep focused on the candidate's ability to do the job. Although only members of protected classes have legal recourse under EEO laws, the regulations help safeguard others by forcing committees to consider only candidates' abilities to do the job.

Search committee members should know that once they consider or ask for unlawful information, then the burden of proof may be on them—not on the applicant—to prove the information was not used to discriminate if a complaint or lawsuit is filed. Because proving the negative is difficult, you need to be sure to avoid prohibited topics in your deliberations and interviews. You know that ignorance of the law is not a valid defense: The results of the employer's action, not the intent, determine if the law has been violated (Gerken, 1993).

Committee members do not always know that by asking seemingly innocent questions such as "Where were you born?" or "What organizations do you belong to?" they are putting their institution at risk. (The question "Where were you born?" reveals national origin and "What organizations do you belong to?" can reveal national origin, religion, race, and other prohibited topics.) For this reason, it is essential to have an HR staff member review the EEO guidelines with all committee members.

Committee members are not only responsible for following EEO guidelines, but also for seeing that all involved with the search do so. The following examples illustrate some ways this can be done.

> If in committee deliberations, one member says, "I know we aren't supposed to consider age, but this guy seems ancient to me," you should quickly respond, "No, we can't consider age." If the committee member's point was that the candidate's educational back-

## EXHIBIT 2.1

### Illegal and Legal Questions

| Inquiry Area | Illegal Questions | Legal Questions |
| --- | --- | --- |
| National Origin/ Citizenship | • Are you a U.S. citizen?<br>• Where were you/your parents born?<br>• What is your "native tongue"? | • Are you authorized to work in the United States?<br>• What languages do you read/speak/write fluently? (This question is okay only if this ability is relevant to the performance of the job.) |
| Age | • How old are you?<br>• When did you graduate?<br>• What's your birth date? | • Are you over the age of 18? |
| Marital/ Family Status | • What's your marital status?<br>• With whom do you live?<br>• Do you plan to have a family? When?<br>• How many kids do you have?<br>• What are your child-care arrangements? | • Would you be willing to relocate if necessary?<br>• Would you be able and willing to travel as needed for the job? (This question is okay if it is asked of all applicants for the job.)<br>• Would you be able and willing to work overtime as necessary? (This question is okay if it is asked of all applicants for the job.) |
| Affiliations | • What clubs or social organizations do you belong to? | • List any professional or trade groups or other organizations you belong to that you consider relevant to your ability to perform this job. |
| Disabilities | • Do you have any disabilities?<br>• Please complete the following medical history . . .<br>• Do you need an accommodation to perform the job? (This question can be asked only after a job offer has been made.) | • Are you able to perform the essential functions of this job? (This question is okay if the interviewer has thoroughly described the job.)<br>• Can you demonstrate how you would perform the following job-related functions? |

*continued*

*continued from previous page*

| Inquiry Area | Illegal Questions | Legal Questions |
|---|---|---|
| Arrest Record | • Have you ever been arrested? | • Have you ever been convicted of _____? (The crime named should be reasonably related to the performance of the job in question.) |
| Military | • If you've been in the military, were you honorably discharged? | • In what branch of the Armed Forces did you serve?<br>• What type of training or education did you receive in the military? |

Source: Adapted from "Handling Illegal Questions" by Rochelle Kaplan (see www.jobweb.com/resources/library/Interviews/Handling_Illegal_46_02.htm). © National Association of Colleges and Employers.

ground is out of date, you could ask about this relevant topic; otherwise change the subject to a BFOQ.

During a campus visit when the candidate is meeting with students, one of the students asks the candidate if she is married. You should quickly intervene and state that it is important for all questions to focus on job qualifications. Refocus the session by calling on another student or asking a question. (Of course, students should be briefed ahead of time about EEO regulations, but we realize that you can't control all behavior.)

During the campus interview, an applicant tells you that her spouse is a chemist and asks about job opportunities in the area. Since the applicant introduced this topic, and it is related to her acceptance of the offer, you can answer her question or refer her to others who can provide information.

In Chapter 6, we discuss additional information on ways to phrase questions on sensitive topics so the focus is job related.

The best defense to a lawsuit is to treat all applicants equally. If committee members or administrators engage in a false search (i.e., they decide whom to hire prior to recruiting), then they are not treating applicants equally and are vulnerable to a lawsuit. Another essential defense is to keep good records of fair employment procedures. Document that you identified the essential job duties and qualifications. Document the reasons for excluding some candidates and selecting others at each stage. By following the steps for conducting an effective search outlined in this book, you will have these records. We provide sample forms illustrating the screening of a file based on established qualifications and forms to record interviews with references and applicants. The reasons for your rejections and selections of candidates should be properly documented, and these forms provide an efficient way to accomplish that documentation.

### Understand Affirmative Action

While equal opportunity regulations and affirmative action (AA) are both designed to eliminate discrimination, they differ substantially in their methods. Affirmative action involves taking specific steps in hiring and promoting to eliminate the current effects of past discrimination and prevent future discrimination. Affirmative action is more complex and controversial than EEO and has been challenged in the courts (see Bernard, 2006 and Kellough, 2006). According to a 2006 special diversity edition of *The Chronicle of Higher Education*, institutions can "face legal risks when they deliberately seek to increase the racial and ethnic diversity" of their faculty and staff, particularly if they do not link their efforts directly to their core mission and if they do not "take a holistic approach when evaluating candidates" (Bernard, 2006, B30–B31). If your institution has an AA policy, refer to Bernard's article for guidance. In addition, have your AA officer explain the policy to the committee and answer any specific questions.

Regardless of whether you are an AA institution or not, we believe your goal must be to create a diverse, strong pool of applicants. This means you need to aggressively recruit candidates with varied backgrounds and perspectives. Chapter 4 provides numerous recommendations for achieving this.

## CONCLUSION

When the search committee is carefully selected and the members know their task and define the procedures and rules they will follow, you have laid a strong foundation for conducting an effective and defensible search. Understanding legal issues is a critical step in the search process and should never be omitted. Thoroughness in the initial stages makes the next steps in hiring right easier.

# Chapter Three

## Define the Job

We have all heard true stories of construction projects where a new wall was supposed to meet an existing one but missed by several feet. Such a debacle happens when accurate blueprints are not drafted and executed. Just as those in construction must have blueprints to guide their work, those conducting searches must have clear plans to guide their efforts. Preparing for your search involves carefully analyzing the position, making several key decisions, and then writing the announcement. This chapter will discuss each of these points.

### ANALYZE THE POSITION

We know many committees skip the step of analyzing the position and go immediately to writing the position announcement. We have one word to say about this: Don't. This would be like a builder beginning construction without a blueprint. Like a blueprint, the position analysis gives you an outline to guide your work. The analysis involves determining 1) the essential duties of the position, 2) the job requirements, which are the "must have" credentials for the position, and 3) the performance criteria, which are those necessary qualifications that must be inferred, such as strong teamwork skills, good writing ability, attention to detail, or supervisory skills.

The analysis does take time initially but saves time later by helping the committee be more proficient and effective. A position analysis can help you to:

- Write a clear and targeted position announcement.

- Screen out candidates more efficiently based on identified job criteria.
- Prepare relevant and legal questions for candidates and references.
- Avoid some contentious committee discussions.
- Avoid wasted time deliberating over irrelevant issues.
- Make defensible, fair decisions.

How does a committee go about the task of analyzing the position? You could talk with those who hold or have held the job and those who have supervised the position; examine existing organizational documents for essential duties; send a questionnaire assessing duties, requirements, and performance criteria to key employees; and rely on the knowledge of committee members.

As the committee reviews the information gathered, members need to make decisions about what truly is vital and what is "nice to have." We urge you to be realistic about the position and as flexible as possible. Clearly, all jobs have certain nonnegotiable requirements and perform- ance criteria necessary for success in the position. Requiring criteria not crucial to the job will limit the pool of applicants and constrain your choices. Consider a college seeking to hire a director of housing. What experience and credentials are truly essential? Is a master's crucial or is a bachelor's with experience sufficient? By requiring the master's degree, the college may unnecessarily limit the number of applicants, thereby closing the door on potentially strong applicants. Similarly, when a his- tory department needs someone to teach Latin American studies, then expertise in Latin American studies is a firm requirement, but the more flexible the department can be about a secondary teaching specialty, the better. When you define your search as broadly as possible, you open the door to a broader range of qualified candidates.

At the same time, avoid being so general in requirements that helpful information is not included for candidates nor is there clear information for decision-making. For example, we see ads for faculty that simply indi- cate the position requires teaching, research, and service. Providing more detailed information will help all involved—for example, if online instruc- tion is required, make clear in your position analysis that candidates need the ability to teach courses using online technology. The position analysis should realistically reflect what is required for success in the position. The essentials must be identified before the announcement is written.

## ESTABLISH INFORMATION NEEDS AND DEADLINES

Before writing the position announcement, you need to decide what candidates should submit in addition to the cover letter, curriculum vitae (CV), and university application, if required. (For some positions, a curriculum vitae or CV is required; for others a résumé or a shortened version of a CV is sufficient. For simplicity, we will use the term CV for both.) The information needed from candidates will vary widely across positions, but we've chosen to discuss three items that are frequently required.

### Letters of Recommendation

Some people argue that letters are meaningless because letter writers only write about positives and don't address difficult issues. But if committee members critically screen letters and ask writers tough questions, letters can be valuable. (For suggestions on how to do this, see Chapters 5 and 6.) Letters and their writers can also provide information about what topics need more exploration and whom to contact for additional information.

We believe the widespread practice of asking for just the names of references without getting letters is unwise. When calling references without having read a letter by them, you have no frame of reference for asking questions and no information on which to build.

### Statement of Philosophy

Some people consider statements of philosophy—teaching, management style, and student success—valuable while others do not. Critics argue that candidates will only voice what they believe is the desired response

---

### EXHIBIT 3.1

#### Plurals of Vita and Curriculum Vitae

The plurals of vita and CV can be confusing for those of us who never learned Latin or have forgotten what we learned. Vitae is plural but curriculum vitae is singular. This is because curriculum is singular, and it is the operative word in CV, not vitae. Curriculum vitae means *course of life* in Latin, and the *ae* on vitae is essentially a modifier meaning *of life*. The plural of curriculum vitae is curricula vitae.

or will compose a philosophy targeted to the type of institution and its perceived needs (e.g., small liberal arts college vs. large research institution). However, others believe these statements provide helpful information about priorities and approaches, particularly if candidates provide supporting examples.

If you require candidates to submit statements of philosophy, use them. Compare the answers of candidates and examine the statements in light of your position analysis. Also, when you interview your top candidates, ask them for specific examples of how they applied their philosophies in their jobs.

### Teaching Portfolio

We have noticed more and more ads requiring candidates for faculty positions to submit teaching portfolios. We believe such portfolios can help the committee assess candidates' abilities in and commitment to teaching. Because not all candidates know what a teaching portfolio should include and because you need to compare all candidates on the same basis, you need to clearly specify what applicants need to submit. For example, the announcement might read:

> The teaching portfolio is to include the following items when available: one page statement of teaching philosophy, all quantitative and narrative student evaluations for the last three years, any supervisor or peer classroom visitation reports, syllabi and major assignments for classes taught in the last three years, and three samples of graded student papers. (This statement is based on an analysis of the usefulness of portfolio elements by Nelson & Olwell, 2002.)

This information could be included in the printed ad or as supplemental information on your unit's web site. Either way, you need to be specific in your request.

### Application Deadline

Decide whether to have a firm application deadline or whether to continue accepting applications until the position is filled. By setting a firm deadline, you encourage potential applicants to apply in a timely fashion and avoid having to continue screening new applications as they are submitted. When you do not set a firm deadline, you must review later applications in the same way as early applications, even if you have already started interviewing. Why choose, then, to leave the deadline open? Sometimes not setting a firm deadline increases your pool of well-qualified candidates so that if initial hiring efforts are unsuccessful, you can avoid re-advertising and save both time and money. If you do not set a firm deadline, we recommend that you specify the date you will begin reviewing applications to encourage early filing.

## WRITE THE POSITION ANNOUNCEMENT

When you peruse ads in *The Chronicle of Higher Education* or other sources, you see a variety of approaches to advertising positions. Some are lengthy and include a comprehensive list of job criteria and much information about the institution; others are short and provide only a minimal job description with a referral to a web site; others are a combination. Providing detailed information in the published announcement is helpful, but you can cut costs significantly by placing a shorter ad. No matter where you advertise or which approach you use, you should describe the position and qualifications, spell out the requirements for applying, be persuasive so qualified candidates will be motivated to apply for the position, and state your institution's commitment to diversity. An ad that does these things well is shown in Exhibit 3.2. Let's look more closely at the components of a good ad.

### Describe the Position and Its Requirements

Since you have analyzed the position, this task should be fairly straight-forward. You need to convey sufficient information so potential applicants can make good decisions about applying. We saw an ad for a dean's position that told potential applicants virtually nothing about the qualifications for the job, only specifying that "we are looking for individuals with demonstrated leadership skills who want to join an outstanding team of administrators, faculty, and staff." The committee for that job no doubt received applications from many who did not meet its requirements and wasted time weeding out those candidates from consideration. Provide more detail about qualifications and save the committee time in the long run. For example, if a Ph.D. is required, say so. Exhibit 3.3 shows an excerpt from an ad that clearly lists duties and qualifications.

EXHIBIT 3.2
_____

**Example of a Well-Prepared Ad**

## Communication Theory Limited-Term Faculty

The Communication Studies Department at the [name of university] invites applications for a limited-term position (up to five years) to begin September 1, 2007. Ph.D. preferred; ABD considered. Teaching responsibilities include three classes per semester from among organizational communication, intercultural communication, small group communication, and communication theory. Creating and teaching courses in an area of specialization is possible. A continuing research program, and clear commitment to active-learning pedagogy and mentoring students, is expected.

Inspired by Catholic tradition, the [university] educates students to be morally responsible leaders who think critically, act wisely, and work skillfully to advance the common good. The successful candidate will possess a commitment to the ideals of this mission statement.

Established in 1885, the [university] is [name of state] largest private university with an enrollment of 11,000 students studying in a wide range of liberal arts, professional, and graduate programs. The University is located in the major metropolitan area of [name of city]. It is within this context of Catholic intellectual tradition and the rich resources of the dynamic, urban [name of city] that [the university] seeks to accomplish our mission of developing individuals who combine career competency with cultural awareness and intellectual curiosity.

The [university] has a strong commitment to the principles of diversity and inclusion, to equal opportunity policies and practices, and to the principles and goals of affirmative action; and, in that spirit, seeks a broad spectrum of candidates who have demonstrated a commitment to these principles. The University strongly encourages nominations of, as well as applications from, women, persons of color, and persons with disabilities.

Send a letter of application (refer to position 200194), curriculum vitae, evidence of teaching excellence, a one-page philosophy of teaching, evidence of an active research program, transcripts, and three letters of recommendation electronically to: [web page] or mail to: [address]. Review of applications will begin December 1, 2006 and continue until the position is filled.

_____

Source: *Spectra,* November 2006, p. 29.

Also, the more specific you can be about job duties, the better. Two examples from *The Chronicle of Higher Education* illustrate how additional information can educate applicants. Rather than simply noting faculty must "conduct research," one ad specified that the successful candidate "is expected to develop a research program involving undergraduates." Another ad clarified that the candidate is to "establish a collaborative research agenda consistent with a Research I university, including the pursuit of external funding." If candidates hate the thought of pursuing grants, you hope they will weed themselves out and save you the trouble.

---

### EXHIBIT 3.3

#### Example of a Clear Statement of Requirements

**Director, School of Music, Associate Professor/Professor**

**Responsibilities:** The director represents the school to all of its constituencies and is responsible for the oversight of degree programs, the budget, long-range planning, faculty recruitment, and development. The director oversees the administrative staff, budget development, and is expected to take a leading role in fundraising. The director is also responsible for promoting the local, national, and international visibility of the school. Candidates must have outstanding leadership, management, and interpersonal skills to relate to a wide diversity of faculty, staff, students and community members.

**Qualifications:** Distinguished record of sustained professional achievement in a music discipline warranting appointment at the rank of associate or full professor with tenure. Advanced degree in music required. The successful candidate will bring to the position:

- Administrative experiences in higher education with evidence of increasing levels of responsibility and accomplishment
- Proven budget management abilities
- Effectiveness in recruitment/retention of faculty and students, strategic planning, and curricular development
- Effective communication and interpersonal abilities
- Successful record of promoting diversity
- Experience in securing external funds
- Experience with faculty/staff evaluation and program development

---

Source: *The Chronicle of Higher Education*, October 6, 2006, p. C25.

We want to again remind you to be as flexible as possible in position requirements. When possible, use words like *should* instead of *must* and *preferred* instead of *required*. Give as much leeway as you can in the job description. Note the flexibility reflected in the following description taken from an ad in the September 2006 issue of *Spectra,* the newsletter of the National Communication Association.

> The successful applicants will teach and develop courses in an area of specialization; examples include, but are not limited to, Relational Communication, Visual Communication, Organizational Communication, or Health Communication.

By conveying the department's ability to be flexible, this ad encourages a wide range of qualified applicants to apply.

## Spell Out the Requirements for Applying

Earlier, the committee made decisions about what to request from applicants. In the ad, make your expectations and needs about what to submit clear to applicants. If you want applicants to submit a statement of philosophy, specify the number of pages. Otherwise you might find yourself wading through 17 pages of drivel. Similarly, if you ask for teaching evaluations, make clear what you want (e.g., all quantitative and qualitative evaluations for the past three years). Be sure to request all evaluations so a candidate cannot select the ones to send. If you request a portfolio, specify exactly what is to be included. If you ask for writing samples, limit pages and consider specifying the type of sample so comparing across candidates will be easier.

## Be Persuasive

In addition to the information about the position, an effective announcement also motivates potential candidates to apply. If your institution is nationally known, then this may not be crucial. Otherwise, decide what will get the attention of candidates who are just skimming announcements. What about the position, institution, or location can be used to convince potential applicants to apply? A few institutions can sell the benefits associated with the position itself, as shown in this excerpt from an ad in *The Chronicle of Higher Education:* "Start up funds, excellent equipment, . . . support for student-faculty research, and a biological field station are available" (October 6, 2006, p. C11). We understand most institutions don't have these benefits to offer. What are the options then? You can highlight major awards received by the institution or give details of the program, such as number of majors. Some stress the attractiveness of the school's location ("clean air, open spaces"). Still others mention salary or excellent fringe benefits such as medical and retirement plans or partner relocation assistance. Note how one university markets itself in this excerpt: "A strong state budget with one of the lowest state tax structures in the nation, and proximity to numerous national parks, recreational areas and forests are among the special fringe benefits" (*The Chronicle of Higher Education*, December 16, 2005).

### Stress Your Institution's Commitment to Diversity

Encourage responses from a wide range of qualified applicants by stressing your institution's commitment to diversity. The standard EOE/AA or EOE notation at the bottom of an ad is so commonplace it has little value. Consider adding a more direct statement to the ad to reflect your institution's mission and practices. Note how this is done in the following excerpts from three ads.

> Johns Hopkins University is an equal opportunity employer committed to recruiting, supporting and fostering a diverse community of outstanding faculty, staff and students. All applicants who share this goal are encouraged to apply. (*Diverse: Issues in Higher Education*, June 1, 2006, p. 116)

> The University of Virginia is an Equal Opportunity/Affirmative Action employer strongly committed to achieving excellence through cultural diversity. The University actively encourages application and nominations from members of underrepresented groups. (*Diverse: Issues in Higher Education*, June 1, 2006, p. 108)

> Plymouth State University is an AA/EEO Employer. We are committed to creating an environment that values and supports diversity, equity and inclusiveness across our campus community and encourage application from qualified individuals who will help us achieve this mission. (*The Chronicle of Higher Education*, October 6, 2006, p. C27)

In her book *Diversifying the Faculty,* Turner (2002) suggests including statements in the announcement that signal your interest in candidates with diverse perspectives. For example, she recommends indicating that you are seeking candidates who have: "Experience with a variety of teaching methods or curricular perspectives," "Interest in developing and implementing curricula that address multicultural issues," or "Demonstrated success in working with diverse populations of students" (pp. 17–18).

## CONCLUSION

Analyzing the position is essential if you want to hire right. The information obtained helps to ensure that you can prepare an effective position announcement, which is needed for successful recruitment, the topic we discuss in the next chapter.

# Chapter Four

## Recruit a Strong Applicant Pool

Picking the best out of a pool of weak applicants doesn't help your unit achieve or maintain excellence. Obviously the chances of a successful hire depend on the quality of applicants. For this reason, you must view recruiting as an active process that involves more than posting an ad in a publication.

### APPEAL TO A WIDE AUDIENCE

Unless you are in the enviable position of knowing that numerous, high-quality, diverse applicants will apply for your position, you need to aggressively recruit such candidates. Adherence to the following recommendations will help you do this.

#### Increase Your Competitiveness

*Advertise early.* We have heard many faculty and administrators lament the poor quality of applications they received for an opening. Yet in almost all of these situations, we know the ad was placed quite late in comparison to other national searches. You can't expect to appeal to top candidates, including highly sought minorities, if you don't get your ad out early. It's simple: If you enter a race late, you can't expect to be competitive. If your unit is genuinely committed to achieving and maintaining excellence and to recruiting diverse faculty, you can't afford to enter after a race has started. You may occasionally be lucky with a late hire, but we believe consistently hiring late will eventually result in the decline of the unit's quality.

Of course, units frequently don't know if a position will be approved until the next year's budget is finalized. However, this should not keep units from advertising as long as there is a good chance of approval; the ad should note that the position is contingent upon funding. If the position isn't funded, you have lost time and the cost of the ad. This is a small price to pay for the chance to be more competitive. Sometimes circumstances such as a late resignation may prohibit advertising early. In these cases, consider a one-year appointment. If this isn't feasible, then you must be especially active in recruiting applicants.

*Make the process user-friendly.* For example, don't ask for official transcripts in the ad: In the early stages, copies should suffice. Similarly, as noted in Chapter 2, be specific about what you ask candidates to submit. If you ask for a managerial philosophy, then specify a one- or two-page limit. Also, if your institution uses or requires an online application process, work with your HR department to avoid duplicating what your unit and HR require.

*Move along quickly.* If a search has long lulls or is put on hold for weeks, expect to lose some of your top candidates who may accept other offers.

### Use Multiple Recruitment Strategies

*Cast as wide a net as possible.* Don't assume an ad in the standard publication for your field (*The Chronicle of Higher Education* or professional newsletter) is sufficient to attract a pool of excellent candidates. Yes, top candidates check *The Chronicle* and professional newsletters, but if candidates are in high demand, you need to do more to get their attention. Consider using the following recruitment avenues:

- Use personal and professional networks to identify top applicants. For example, ask deans or department chairs of graduate programs to recommend students whose interests are consistent with those of your institution, and then contact those students directly. Also, ask those deans and department chairs to suggest others who are in a good position to recommend strong candidates. Don't perpetuate the old-boy network by relying only on your own personal network of friends.
- Send announcements to targeted graduate schools, including those with excellent reputations, that are nearby, emphasize the teaching skills of graduate students, or graduate many minorities.

- Use electronic sources such as listservs and online postings. Post your announcement on your unit's web site.
- Interview and network at national conferences that large groups of applicants are likely to attend.
- Interview and network at regional conferences where the opportunity for personal interaction may be greater than at national conventions.

*Personally recruit top applicants.* Good recruitment is an ongoing, cumulative process; all employees in a unit should be on the lookout for excellent candidates all the time. When positions open, unit members should reach out and urge them to apply. Frequently candidates will apply to a school they might not otherwise consider just because they receive a personal invitation.

*View communication with applicants as a recruiting tool.* All of your written and oral messages to applicants do more than impart information. Some messages serve to encourage and persuade. Others serve to build a positive relationship by letting candidates know you are professional and value their applications.

After you receive an application, promptly send a letter of acknowledgement, letting the applicant know you are pleased that he or she has applied and providing some persuasive information. All too often these letters of acknowledgement are cold and mechanical, as the following example illustrates.

> As Chair of the Search Committee, I am acknowledging receipt of your application materials. At this time, your application is complete. (Or your application is incomplete and the following material is missing. If you wish to be considered, please submit all missing material no later than October 29.) We appreciate your interest in this position.

The example that follows is a letter of acknowledgement that sends a different message of interest and friendliness and includes helpful and persuasive information applicants might not know.

> I was pleased to receive your application for _____. At this time your application is complete. (Or your application is incomplete and the following material is missing. Please be sure we have all missing material no later than October 29.)

On our web site _____, you will find information about our department, college, and community. We are a small under-graduate department with five full-time and four part-time faculty and 200 majors. Our department student/teacher ratio is 15:1. We value and reward effective teaching and work closely with our students to help ensure their success.

For the last five years, *U.S. News & World Report* has recognized our college as one of the top private colleges in the South. On the web site you will find other awards the college has won and much more information about us.

Please visit the web site _____ for photographs and information on the local community. You will see the community has much to offer and the college is fortunate to be in such a prime location.

I appreciate your interest in teaching for us. Deliberations will begin after October 29, and I will be in touch when the committee has completed its initial screening. If you have any questions, please don't hesitant to contact me.

The writer of the second letter uses the opportunity to persuade candidates to remain interested in the position and seek more information. People usually don't hesitate to use this type of persuasion in person; yet for some reason they don't do so in the initial letter of acknowledgement, which is a wasted opportunity. You should also consider sending a department or university brochure with the letter. If a candidate has applied to 15 schools and you are the only one who has sent an inviting, warm letter, then your letter should help you be more competitive.

After the letter of acknowledgment, continue to have ongoing, prompt contact with the candidates. Don't leave them in the dark about what is happening. Be honest. For example, if they are not in your top group but are being held in reserve, tell them (see the sample letter in Appendix B). If you have a change in the anticipated timetable, be sure to inform the remaining applicants.

Treating all candidates well from the beginning to the end of the process will help recruiting in the long run. Treating applicants poorly, even the ones you are not interested in, only hurts your reputation. Word gets around, and others may be discouraged from applying for a position at your school. Frequently we read items in *The Chronicle of Higher Education* written by job applicants describing shabby treatment in

---

EXHIBIT 4.1
_____

**Strategies for Developing a Strong Candidate Pool**

- Advertise as early as possible.
- Make the application process as user-friendly as feasible.
- Move the search along quickly.
- Cast as wide a net as possible.
- Personally recruit top applicants.
- View communication with applicants as a recruiting tool.

---

searches. Similarly, some top minority applicants described searches they experienced as "inhumane" processes that left them "feeling unappreciated" (Smith, 2000). We don't believe the majority of search committee chairs intentionally dispense such treatment: It occurs for other reasons such as being disorganized, getting busy and failing to notify candidates, or sending sterile formula letters that have been used for decades. Viewing all communication with candidates as part of recruiting will help send a positive message and keep you competitive.

## APPEAL TO A DIVERSE AUDIENCE

Most colleges and universities are committed to the value of diversity and to creating a diverse learning environment. (For discussions of the benefits of diversity in higher education, see Smith & Moreno, 2006; Turner, 2002; Umbach & Kuh, 2006.) Student bodies are becoming more and more diverse. According to projections from the National Center for Education Statistics (Hussar & Bailey, 2006), by the year 2015 well over half of all new college students will be from currently underrepresented populations including African Americans, Hispanics, Pacific Islanders, Native Americans, and Asians. The profile of the student population has changed significantly over the last 14 years (Hussar & Bailey, 2006), yet the demographics of the faculty have not changed accordingly (e.g., see Knapp et al., 2005; Trower & Chait, 2002; Turner, 2002; Wilson, 2003). The number of women in some positions and disciplines has increased significantly, but they are still underrepresented in some areas (Fogg, 2006).

Faculty and staff need to be a good representation of the student body and wider community. If only 3% of a college faculty is African American in a community comprised of 30% African Americans, the institution is sending a negative message to both blacks and whites about the role of people of color in higher education. If few faculty in science are women, then this sends a message to males and females about women's role in science. Similarly, if the entire faculty in elementary education or nursing is female, this also sends a message about the role of men in these fields. (We realize men in these fields do not meet the legal definition of minorities, but they are nonetheless an underrepresented group.)

Your goal is to recruit faculty and staff who will contribute to the excellence and diversity of the campus. The commitment to diversity cannot be separated from the focus on excellence. Indeed, having a diverse faculty and staff is one important step toward excellence.

If diversity is a real value and not just an expressed one, institutions must aggressively recruit applicants from historically underrepresented groups. Let's consider some of the things you can do to attract a diverse applicant pool.

### Follow the Earlier Recommendations

Advertising early and moving the search along, casting as wide a net as possible, personally recruiting top applicants, and viewing communication with applicants as part of recruiting will help you attract highly sought top minority candidates. For example, extending personal invitations to top minority candidates can make a huge difference in whether they apply. You might think such applicants would receive numerous invitations, but a study conducted by Claremont Graduate University found otherwise (Smith, 2000). All in a unit should use their personal and professional networks to locate excellent candidates from underrepresented groups and urge them to apply. Look over your list of alumni for candidates to contact. In searching for applicants to invite to apply, you could also consult the *Minority and Women Doctoral Directory*, an up-to-date registry of thousands of candidates who have recently received, or are soon to receive, a doctorate or master's degree. A campus can buy the entire directory or a unit can pay to consult the roster for candidates in its discipline.

### Don't Assume Minority Candidates Are Unavailable to You

A research team at Claremont Graduate University surveyed top minority job candidates to study the treatment they received in the job market.

The research team selected the most desirable candidates—former Ford, Mellon, and Spencer Fellowship recipients who had completed their Ph.D.s. The team discovered that it is a myth to assume top minority applicants are unavailable to most institutions. Although minority candidates are scarce in some disciplines, the Claremont study participants expressed interest in different positions, regions, and institutional types. Some minority candidates wished to locate in a certain geographical area for personal reasons and expressed regret at not being recruited at regional institutions in the area (Smith, 2000). More recently, Turner (2002) and Smith and Moreno (2006) argued that the unavailability of minority candidates is a myth used as an excuse for not hiring minorities.

## Use Multiple Recruitment Strategies

*Advertise in sources aimed at reaching diverse populations.* In addition to *The Affirmative Action Registry* (the national EEO recruitment publication), consider advertising in magazines such as *Diverse: Issues in Higher Education* (the former *Black Issues in Higher Education)* and *Hispanic Outlook in Higher Education,* which both include ads in the magazines as well as online job postings. Search for minority associations in your field and see if they offer a career center. For example, if you were searching for an engineering professor, you could place ads with the Society of Mexican American Engineers and Scientists and the Society of Women Engineers.

Regardless of your discipline, you could also place your ad with one of the national minority recruitment firms. The National Employment Minority Network (www.nemnet.com) is a national resource organization committed to assisting in the recruitment of minority students and professionals. It posts academic jobs on its web site and gathers vitae from minority professionals. IMDiversity (www.imdiversity.com) is a recruitment and placement firm whose purpose is to provide career information to minorities, specifically African Americans, Asian Americans, Hispanic Americans, Native Americans, and women.

*Send notices to colleges and universities with high proportions of minority students,* particularly ones with a reputation for a strong degree program in the needed field and ones in your geographical region.

*Contact organizations that serve underrepresented groups.* For example, most professional organizations have caucuses for minorities and women. You could contact the officers of the caucus and ask for recommendations of candidates or ask for help in disseminating your ad.

---

EXHIBIT 4.2

### Be Proactive About Recruiting a Diverse Applicant Pool

- Follow the recommendations for developing a strong candidate pool.
- Don't assume minority candidates are unavailable to you.
- Advertise in sources aimed at reaching diverse populations.
- Send notices to colleges and universities with high proportions of minority students.
- Contact organizations that serve underrepresented groups.
- Foster respect for diversity on your campus.
- Seek those who value diversity.

---

## Demonstrate Your Commitment to Diversity

*Foster respect for diversity on campus.* If respect for diversity is only an expressed value and is not embedded in the institutional mission and practices, then even the best recruitment strategies will fail. An institution must focus on having a campus climate that values diversity and equity. Your reputation is your best recruitment tool.

*Seek those who value diversity.* Promoting a climate of inclusiveness involves more than hiring those from underrepresented groups. You also need to hire those who agree with the benefits of diversity to your institution and students. Seek candidates who have a record of successfully working with a variety of people (e.g., Fulbright scholars, Peace Corp workers, Pew Hispanic Center grantees).

## FOLLOW GOOD PRACTICES FOR RETAINING EMPLOYEES

Recruitment and retention are inextricably linked. If newly hired faculty and staff do not feel welcomed and appreciated when they come to campus, then you will have a retention problem. If recent hires leave, word will then spread and make additional recruitment of top candidates, including highly sought minorities, more difficult.

Although exploration of practices designed to increase retention (such as mentoring for new employees, offering faculty and staff development programs, accommodating special needs, and providing opportunities to develop courses and programs in the area of specialization) are beyond the scope of this book, we want to stress that such practices are directly related to an institution's ability to recruit top candidates.

In addition, campus administrators need to monitor problems that affect the retention of all employees. This is particularly important with diverse employees who frequently report problems such as feelings of isolation, lack of appreciation, and lack of campus interest in diversity. One important tool in discovering retention problems is conducting exit interviews with all departing employees. Although this tool should be used for all employees, these interviews are crucial for uncovering obstacles faced by minorities and women.

## CONCLUSION

To hire right, you need to have a diverse pool of strong candidates. In this chapter, we offered a series of recommendations to help you recruit effectively, including suggestions for reaching underrepresented groups. When you have done a thoughtful and thorough job of recruiting, you should have a good pool of applicants and can begin the process of systematically evaluating candidates.

# Chapter Five

## Evaluate
## Candidate Files

After candidate materials are submitted and logged, search committee members must begin the difficult and important task of evaluating candidate files. As you undertake this task, remember that a candidate's file is in essence a sales brochure. No one expects candidates to openly discuss potential problems in their files. Candidates prepare their materials to emphasize strengths and downplay shortcomings. The file is basically an advertisement designed to create interest and entice you to view the candidate as a possible match for your position. When buying a car, you realize a brochure does not contain all the information you need to know, so you must critically examine what is written and what is not, and then gather additional information. In the search process, you must also critically examine the candidate's materials and eventually verify the information by conducting interviews and checking references, as we will discuss in the next chapter.

In addition to looking critically at candidate materials, you need to have a well-defined way to systematically evaluate candidates. Over the years, we have heard plenty of complaints from colleagues and friends about how candidates are evaluated. We've worked with those who judged candidates primarily on the school attended, a shared interest, or the stature of a letter writer. We've heard stories about committees that failed to define criteria for evaluating candidates in advance so that decision-making was nearly impossible. To avoid these kinds of problems, help committees be efficient and effective, and help ensure the search is fair and defensible, the evaluation must be carefully planned and systematically carried out. In this chapter, we offer recommendations for evaluating candidate files, beginning with materials prepared by the candidate, then letters of recommendation, and lastly a few cautions.

## DEVELOP AN EVALUATION FORM

In Chapter 3 we discussed the process of examining the job and defining the performance factors associated with success in the job. As you will recall, the job requisites are "must have" items, such as an earned Ph.D. in a given discipline or a certain number of years of supervisory experience. Performance criteria are qualifications that must be inferred, such as strong interpersonal skills, managerial effectiveness, flexibility, or ability to work on a team. Committee members need to keep focused on these qualifications as they evaluate files, so we strongly recommend developing an evaluation form that reiterates the job requisites and performance criteria and is consistent with the job analysis and the published ad.

The evaluation form should be straightforward, thorough, and easy to use. It should have space at the top for the candidate's name or ID number, the evaluator's name, and the date. Some committees record only last names or use code numbers to lessen the chances of gender or ethnic bias. Committee members should use the form to record ratings and take notes as they review candidate files so they are reminded of the critical performance factors as they review and later discuss files. Let's take a closer look.

Exhibit 5.1 shows an advertisement that clearly delineates the requisites and criteria for the position of vice president of student life.

In accordance with the ad, each requirement and performance criterion should also be listed on the evaluation form. In the case of the vice president of student life, the form would include degree, years of experience, written communication skills, interpersonal skills, and so on. Requirements that committee members have agreed are job requisites should be listed first and have a yes/no option for evaluating the candidate (as noted in Chapter 2). Anyone without the requisites is eliminated from further consideration. After the requisites, list the performance criteria and include any rating scale previously chosen by the committee. Be sure to provide space for committee members to comment on each criterion. This will be important later when individuals share their ratings with the committee and need to defend their positions. Finally, provide space at the bottom of the form for any additional comments and for the overall rating of the candidate (e.g., *yes, no, maybe*). A sample

---

EXHIBIT 5.1
---

**Advertisement for Position of Vice President of Student Life**

**Position Description:** The Vice President of Student Life serves as the chief administrative officer overseeing the planning, development, implementation, and coordination of a comprehensive student development program providing leadership for a variety of student life departments, programs, and services that enhance the quality of life for a diverse university population.

**Qualifications:**
- Earned doctorate degree
- Five years of demonstrated success and progressively responsible administrative experience in higher ed/student affairs (Preference given to: senior level experience and with experience in two or more of the areas of responsibility)
- Strong written, oral, and interpersonal communication skills
- Collaborative style of leadership conducive to working effectively with various internal and external constituencies within the context of a strong shared governance system
- Demonstrated experience in strategic planning and in fiscal and resource planning, allocation, and management
- Demonstrated ability to partner effectively across divisions to create programs that provide positive learning experiences for students
- Evidence of personal involvement in the life of a campus
- Ability to develop excellent rapport with students
- Demonstrated experience in working with diverse student and staff populations

---

Source: *The Chronicle of Higher Education,* December 16, 2005, p. C64.

---

form based on the ad for vice president of student life is shown in Exhibit 5.2 and a simpler evaluation form for a faculty search is shown in Exhibit 5.3.

## SYSTEMATICALLY AND CRITICALLY REVIEW THE FILES

Now that you have a well-designed evaluation form, you are ready to evaluate the files. Knowing that files are put together to serve as sales

EXHIBIT 5.2

## Candidate Evaluation Form (Vice President of Student Life)

Candidate Name_____ Evaluated by_____ Date_____

### Job Requisites

Yes    No    Earned Ph.D.

Yes    No    Five years experience in higher ed/student affairs

Yes    No    Experience in strategic planning

Yes    No    Experience in fiscal and resource planning, allocation,
              and management

Yes    No    Experience with diverse student/staff populations

### Performance Criteria

1    2    3    4    5    Senior level experience

1    2    3    4    5    Experience in two or more areas of responsibility

1    2    3    4    5    Degree of success in former roles

1    2    3    4    5    Extent to which responsibilities increased

1    2    3    4    5    Written communication skills

1    2    3    4    5    Oral communication skills

1    2    3    4    5    Interpersonal communication skills

1    2    3    4    5    Collaborative leadership style

1    2    3    4    5    Effectiveness with internal/external constituencies

1    2    3    4    5    Effectiveness in shared governance system

1    2    3    4    5    Ability to create effective learning programs across
                         divisions

1    2    3    4    5    Personal involvement in life of campus

1    2    3    4    5    Rapport with students

### Comments_____

_____

### Overall Rating

Yes    Maybe    No

EXHIBIT 5.3

## Candidate Evaluation Form (Assistant Professor of Sociology)

**Candidate Name**_____ **Evaluated by**_____ **Date**_____

**Current Position**

**Job Requisites**

Yes   No   Earned Ph.D. If not, evidence that Ph.D. will be completed by August.

Year conferred_____ Specialization_____

Yes   No   Experience teaching Intro to Sociology

Yes   No   Ability to teach classes in needed specialization [list areas here]

**Performance Criteria**

1. Teaching

    A. Courses which have been or could be taught by candidate

    B. Evidence of teaching effectiveness

2. Scholarship/Research Area(s)

    Presentations/publications

    Potential for meeting Research I standards

3. Communication Skills

    A. Evidence of written skills

    B. Evidence of oral skills

4. Commitment to Diversity

**Comments**_____

_____

**Overall Rating**

Yes      Maybe      No

brochures, good evaluators scrutinize what messages are actually written as well as decipher oblique messages. They examine the total package of materials to determine what is stressed and what is not stressed in the file documents.

### Evaluate Candidate-Prepared Material

Before discussing questions to ask about each file, we want to emphasize two common problems to watch for in candidate-prepared materials. One is the possibility that candidates did not write their own CVs and cover letters, and the other is that candidates have inflated their CVs and have in essence written a deceptive ad.

We conducted a quick Internet search for companies that help job applicants prepare CVs and cover letters. In less than a minute, we had URLs for dozens of companies. One company guaranteed a job interview, another touted "certified professional résumé writers" who would present "personal information in a culturally sensitive way," and yet another had "content experts" who "focus on creating content" for job applicants. If these "hired hands" write a candidate's cover letter and CV, then the task of validly assessing organizational and communication skills is more difficult but not impossible when you inspect the entire package for consistency. If the writers (whether candidates or hired hands) "create content," meaning they exaggerate, pad, or fabricate, then the task is also more difficult.

Unfortunately, vita inflation is a very real problem. Note the widely publicized case of Notre Dame football coach George O'Leary who claimed on his CV that he played football at the University of New Hampshire and received a master's degree from New York University. In fact, he had done neither. Five days after O'Leary was hired at Notre Dame, his lies surfaced and he resigned in embarrassment (ESPN.com, 2001). No doubt members of the hiring committee were also embarrassed. And O'Leary's case is not an isolated one. In 2002, the president of Albright College abruptly resigned after it was revealed he claimed to be the author of two books that did not exist (Basinger, 2004). A survey reported in *Time* indicated that 44% of résumés contained lies or exaggerations (Kluger, 2002). Vita inflation is too common to ignore and is one of many reasons why those involved in hiring must carefully scrutinize all information in the file. As you read, make note on the evaluation form of items needing verification.

The following are questions you should ask when reviewing all candidate-prepared documents (e.g., cover letter, CV, teaching philosophy). Some questions are obvious and some are not. Some require you to read between the lines, some to critically evaluate words and phrases. In our discussion, we indicate that some information in the file should be flagged for later investigation. Most of the flagged items are not grounds for rejecting a candidate, and potentially negative information should not exclude candidates who have an otherwise strong record. Flagging only means you need to check out the information, just as you would verify degrees and interview references for all your most qualified candidates. If something in the file should be flagged, the reviewer should make note of it on the evaluation form.

*Does the candidate have the needed skills, abilities, and experience for the position?* The evaluation sheet containing the performance criteria should be before you as you review the files and carefully assess the extent to which the candidates provide evidence that they meet the criteria.

*Is the material well written?* Regardless of the discipline, you should expect good writing: After all, this is a position in higher education. If the candidate submits materials with serious writing and spelling errors, you cannot expect that person to write cogent documents for your unit, compose clear and credible emails, or effectively develop the writing skills of students or subordinates.

*Is the quality of writing consistent throughout the file?* If candidates have prepared their own materials, the quality and style of writing should be consistent throughout the file. A well-written cover letter coupled with a poorly written managerial philosophy should be a flag. We know of a recent incident where the writing in the candidate's cover letter was significantly better than in the rest of the file. An Internet search indicated entire parts of the cover letter had been lifted from samples of letters available on the Internet.

*Is the material well planned?* All material should show a candidate has been thoughtful, thorough, and careful and has targeted the submitted materials to show his or her fit with your position. Professionalism is a reasonable expectation.

*Is the material persuasive?* A strong file contains compelling arguments and evidence. For example, the cover letter should indicate a candidate's knowledge of and interest in your position. It should give you a good idea of an individual's communication skills, goals, and suitability for your position and make you want to read the rest of the file. The remainder of the file should provide support for the arguments in the cover letter. Similarly, if you ask for a teaching portfolio, look for evidence in syllabi and course assignments that supports what a candidate avows as a teaching philosophy. When analyzing an entire file, give weight to specific and concrete evidence.

*Are accomplishments discussed in specific terms or in vague generalities?* The language a candidate uses to describe accomplishments is important. For example, phrases like *served on* and *participated in* are red flags because they are vague and may indicate a lack of substantive involvement in activities. We all probably have served on committees with people who did little but show up for meetings, so reviewers must look for specific examples of contributions. Also be wary of words such as *studied* and *familiar with*. Without more information, you don't know if the candidate has extensive knowledge or has merely read a book on the subject. Likewise, long lists of responsibilities without concomitant accomplishments are worrisome because every employee has responsibilities, but not all have noteworthy accomplishments.

*Are job titles and responsibilities reasonable for the candidate to have achieved at the given time?* In 2005, it was revealed that Michael Brown, the former head of the Federal Emergency Management Agency (FEMA), was guilty of résumé padding. According to his online profile and official bio on the FEMA web site, he served as "an assistant city manager with emergency services oversight" in Edmond, Oklahoma. When reporters contacted the officials in Edmond, they discovered Brown was an "assistant to the city manager . . . not a manager himself, and had no authority over other employees" (Fonda & Healy, 2005). Because Brown held the position when he was a college student and had no previous administrative experience, a discerning reviewer should have questioned whether he could have been an assistant city manager considering his background. Critical reviewers scrutinize credentials for such discrepancies.

*Do job responsibilities and accomplishments match the job title?* We reviewed a CV once where an instructor reported carrying out duties typically handled by a department chair. This is the sort of imbalance that may suggest vita inflation. Committees might also see an opposite scenario. Envision a former dean who now lists on the CV an impressive title but few substantive responsibilities. One might wonder if the dean was asked to resign and was appeased with an impressive new title. To be fair to the candidate and your institution, flag the information and follow up if the candidate's credentials are otherwise strong.

*Are the applicant's organizational memberships meaningful?* Memberships in organizations or positions on boards do not equate to action. Put simply, a long listing of memberships without specific accomplishments is meaningless.

*Is basic information easily accessible?* The organization of the CV can indicate how well organized the applicant is and whether information might be purposely hidden. Educational history, for example, should be listed so that institutions, degrees, and major areas of study are easily found. Dates of employment should be obvious. Gaps should be flagged.

*Has the candidate been at numerous schools for only a few years each?* Look for an ongoing record of commitment and effectiveness. Frequent job relocations may or may not indicate such a record. For example, one candidate may have changed positions frequently because she could not get along with colleagues; another may have moved because of family obligations. Still another candidate may have left a position after five years because he was a poor performer who was denied tenure; another may have left because he was offered a more challenging position. Don't assume. Verify.

*Is the degree-granting institution accredited by an independent and credible agency?* If you have never heard of an institution, flag it to be checked. Further, look at the names of degree-granting institutions closely. Many diploma mills take names similar to highly credible institutions. Consider the example of Trinity University and College, which is not affiliated with Trinity University in San Antonio or any of the Trinity Colleges in the United States or England. Rather, it is a small self-accredited institution that publicizes that one can get a degree without courses or examinations (see www.trinityeducation.com).

According to a 2006 ABC News report, congressional investigators discovered that 463 federal employees had bogus degrees from unaccredited schools. Certainly higher education is not exempt from counterfeit claims, and you need to authenticate when in doubt. The Federal Trade Commission has a publication available to help identify fake degrees (see www.ftc.gov/opa/2005/02/diplomamills.htm).

Critical review of applicants' credentials is a crucial step in hiring right. The suggestions offered here should help you systematically evaluate the files to identify the best candidates for your positions.

---

EXHIBIT 5.4

**Checklist for Evaluating Candidate Files**

✔ Does the candidate have the needed skills, abilities, and experience for the position?
✔ Is the material well written?
✔ Is the quality of writing consistent throughout the file?
✔ Is the material well planned?
✔ Is the material persuasive?
✔ Are accomplishments discussed in specific terms or in vague generalities?
✔ Are job titles and responsibilities reasonable for the candidate to have achieved at the given time?
✔ Do job responsibilities and accomplishments match the job title?
✔ Are the applicant's organizational memberships meaningful?
✔ Is basic information easily accessible?
✔ Has the candidate been at numerous schools for only a few years each?
✔ Is the degree-granting institution accredited by an independent and credible agency?

---

## Evaluate Letters of Recommendation

Reference letters are similar to eulogies. Both are "speeches of praise" designed to focus on the positive and overlook the negative. We rarely have reason to analyze eulogies, but for reference letters to be helpful, readers must remember they are written as speeches of praise and must scrutinize them carefully.

Some argue that letters of recommendation are of little value, but by knowing what to expect in these documents of praise, you will be able to evaluate them effectively and obtain useful information. You know to expect some exaggeration—for example, satisfactory performance becomes good and good becomes outstanding. (When is the last time you read or wrote a reference letter that claimed an applicant's performance was average?) You know not to expect candor about potential problems because this is not the purpose of the letter. Indeed, you should expect letter writers to avoid unpleasant issues or even obfuscate to conceal weaknesses.

In spite of expectations of exaggeration and evasion, we don't think the vast majority of letter writers outright lie. Yes, professors want their students to get jobs, but they also want to maintain their credibility, and they can't know for sure who will read their letters. Friends of candidates want them to find employment, so they will be generous with praise, but facts can be checked and references called so we believe it is rare for letter writers to fabricate details.

We have talked to many people about letters they wrote for less than satisfactory students or employees. Even though no one wrote anything blatantly negative, most expected that an astute reviewer could attend to what was said, reading between the lines to find the implied message. The writers felt they had done their duty; now it was up to the reviewer to read critically.

An additional concern regarding letters of recommendation is the use of "canned" letters. Even though the majority of references may write their own letters, all do not craft a *new* letter for each candidate. Some have a canned letter they use for everyone. Others use letters they have purchased from web sites that sell packages of sample letters. There are scores of web sites advertising that buyers can choose from dozens of professionally written letters (e.g., www.a1recommendationletters.com) and that appropriate phrases and sentences can be easily copied and pasted into a letter (e.g., www.instantrecommendationletterkit.com). However, using such references rarely produces good letters because specific details are missing, and the critical reviewer will note the lack of supporting examples.

In sum, we believe a review of letters is more helpful than many think *as long as* the letters are critically examined. You can learn much if you look for specific information, examine how the praise is given, and notice what is *not* said.

To help you scrutinize letters, we recommend one reference review sheet for each candidate (see Exhibit 5.5). The sheet contains a summary of your evaluation of the letters and your answers to questions about the letters. Although completing the sheet takes time, it saves time in the long run by eliminating the need to go through letters again. You should ask the questions presented next, unless of course, you can tell from examining a CV that a candidate does not have the needed credentials to even be considered.

*Are the letters from key people?* Before inspecting the contents of the letters, look at who wrote them. Letter writers should have worked closely with applicants so they can provide details about the applicants' work. At least one letter should be from a supervisor. Look at the refer-

---

EXHIBIT 5.5

### Sample Form for Evaluating Reference Letters

**Review of Reference Letters**

Candidate_____

List the positions of those writing the letters.

Which performance criteria are emphasized?

Which are not?

Did the writers support opinions with facts? Note any compelling
   evidence cited.

Note any potential red flags in the letters.

Who else needs to be contacted for a phone interview?

Summary comments

---

ences and see if key people are missing without a logical explanation. For example, if a person is a team member of an important project, then at least one letter should be from a team member. If a person has had several recent positions, some letters should be from previous supervisors. If key people did not write, make note on the review sheet. For candidates who become finalists, you can contact key people when you have obtained the candidates' permission to do so.

*Which performance criteria are emphasized? Which are not?* Examine the letters and note the qualifications that are and are not stressed. For example, is the quality of teaching emphasized? Ability to conduct research? Budgetary acumen? Communication competence? If all letter writers stress an applicant's teaching effectiveness, the message sent is that teaching effectiveness is important to the applicant. Likewise, if no writers discuss teaching, the letters send a different message that warrants follow-up. On the review sheet, record which criteria are emphasized, such as quality of scholarship, success in fundraising and alumni development, and organizational skills as an administrator. Be sure also to note which of the performance criteria are *not* mentioned in the letters. Keep in mind some letter writers may seem very positive, but upon careful review you will discover that the writer did not mention any of the performance criteria deemed important for a particular job. Indeed, we both admit to writing letters where we deliberately did not mention key performance criteria. A few times in the past when we felt obligated to write recommendations for advisees who wanted to go to graduate school but were weak students, we wrote letters focusing on attributes such as congeniality, enthusiasm, hard work, and commitment. We wrote honest, positive letters, but avoided discussing how well we thought they would do in graduate school.

*Are opinions supported with facts?* Examine the letters for specific details and pay more attention to the details than to unsupported praise. If a writer claims a person is greatly admired on campus, then the letter and the candidate's CV should contain evidence to support this. Examples of evidence could be awards received or invitations to serve on important committees. If a major professor maintains that a student is one of the best she has ever taught in 20 years of teaching, then the letter or CV should certainly contain support for this claim. If not, be suspicious. Of course, some claims cannot be supported with evidence, but good letters should contain more facts than opinions. On the review sheet, note the evidence provided by the writers. Remember, someone can be damned with faint praise or saved by compelling support of superior performance.

*Are any red flags raised in the letters?* Inspect the letters for any red flags and note them on the review sheet. Writers rarely wave red flags to identify problems; usually you have to search for them. Most writers want to be honest without saying anything blatantly negative, so one strategy for finding flags is to look carefully at what the writer actually says. One of us once read a letter for an applicant who held a temporary teaching position. A colleague in the candidate's department wrote: "If we had a permanent position, _____ would be considered for it." At the least, search committee members expected an enthusiastic writer to say that the applicant would be a strong candidate for the position, so they took this statement to be a red flag. The tone of this letter and the other references were lukewarm, and as a result the candidate did not make the *yes* group.

What a writer does not say can also be a red flag. For example, if a major professor writes eloquently about a student's enthusiasm, confidence, and desire to succeed but never mentions the quality of the student's work, this suggests a problem. If two letter writers mention an individual's independent spirit and never discuss anything related to collegiality, then they are probably warning you that the person "does not play well with others."

The words writers choose might also raise flags. Look for words that can have different meanings. For instance, claiming a candidate has "good potential" can be praise or criticism depending on the context. If a letter writer commends a candidate who has been teaching for three years for her enormous teaching potential, this could mean the writer thinks her teaching performance is poor. Words such as *solid, diligent,* and *hardworking* can also be used to compliment or denigrate. If such descriptive adjectives are used without concomitant praise for the work of a candidate, they are red flags. Just as you did with the CV, watch for code words such as *participated in, familiar with,* and *good effort.* If a writer notes that a candidate participated in a certain educational program, you have learned nothing about the *quality* of the participation. An occasional use of such terms may not be negative, but if the letter is otherwise lukewarm and lacks specifics, then the language may be used intentionally and you should take note.

Unfortunately, we can't provide a list of code words that signal problems because the context in which words are used determines their meaning. But be on the lookout for words with several meanings and for hidden messages sent by writers. At the same time, be fair to candidates and look for evidence that is contrary to your negative interpretation. Not all references are good writers and not all choose words with care, so you should be careful not to assume hidden meanings in any one message. You are looking for evidence to screen candidates in and out, so you want to consider the cumulative message sent by all the writers.

Sometimes this critical review of letters will provide enough information to help screen a candidate in or out. Other times it will not, but the review should let you know what candidate qualifications you need to examine in more detail. Then you can use the information to compose questions for interviews with candidates and references.

## Heed Three Cautions

We've noted the need to be aware of the choices candidates make in preparing materials. In this final section, we want to caution you about potential perceptual errors we can make as reviewers.

*Recognize cultural differences in persuasive styles.* Committee members need to recognize that persuasive styles are culturally determined and influence how candidates present themselves on paper. In the dominant U.S. culture, job applicants are told that the CV is not the place to be

---

EXHIBIT 5.6
_____

**Checklist for Evaluating Reference Letters**

✔ Are the letters from key people?
✔ Which performance criteria are emphasized? Which are not?
✔ Are opinions supported with facts?
✔ Are any red flags raised in the letters?

---

modest; rather, they should assertively sell themselves and explicitly stress their strengths.

Yet this advice goes against the cultural norms learned by many Asians and Africans (e.g., Hall, 2005). Some applicants who realize the difference in cultural norms attempt to follow U.S. norms in their job search but have difficulty doing so. For example, a few years ago one of our search committees received an application from a native Korean who had just received her terminal degree in the United States. She used the phrases: "I am wise . . . I am a great teacher and students like me much." For most U.S. natives, this language is awkward and boastful. U.S. natives would not usually write, "I am a great teacher." Instead they would give specifics, such as "My student evaluations are consistently above the mean," to lead readers to the conclusion. The difference in directly selling yourself and being boastful is a linguistic nuance that is hard to learn, and reviewers should generally not penalize those from other cultures who fail to grasp this subtlety. Nor should we automatically penalize those who follow the norms of their culture and present abilities in more indirect and modest ways.

Candidates from still other cultures, such as ones found in Greece and many Arabic nations, tend to be more direct than the native U.S. culture, and they may also encounter problems (e.g., Broome, 2000; Ting-Toomey & Chung, 2005). If they do not adjust their language style, some reviewers may perceive them as bragging or embellishing.

In some positions, such as public relations or international business, employees need to understand the linguistic subtleties and rules of the dominant U.S. culture, but in many positions, this is not the case. If committee members are insensitive to cultural norms, they may lose good candidates. To avoid this, focus on specific accomplishments while recognizing different norms in persuasive styles.

---

EXHIBIT 5.7

### Avoiding Perceptual Errors

- Be aware of cultural differences in persuasive styles.
- Avoid the tendency to overemphasize the negative.
- Be cautious of selecting candidates in your own image.

---

*Recognize the tendency to focus on the negative.* Humans have a strong perceptual tendency to give excess attention to even small amounts of negative information. (See Kellerman, 1989, for information on the negativity effect.) Sometimes the negative information is significant, and a candidate is quickly rejected. However, other times search committee members can let one negative item outweigh an otherwise strong record. Keep in mind that every candidate has weaknesses. If you reject too quickly, you may overlook a qualified applicant. Use the evaluation sheet to help make a balanced and fair judgment.

*Recognize the tendency to select in your own image.* Many people look for others who possess attributes and perspectives similar to their own. After all, our own attributes have usually served us well. Further, we tend to like people who are like us. (For information on the similarity thesis, see Adler, Rosenfeld, & Proctor, 2007.) But hiring a clone does not strengthen a unit. Diverse experiences and perspectives (provided they are logical and appropriately voiced) are necessary for the long-term vitality of a unit.

## CONCLUSION

We can't stress enough the importance of critically and systemically evaluating the files based on job requisites and performance criteria. By developing a standardized form for judging and rating candidate materials and knowing how to scrutinize the materials, individual committee members can do a better job of screening candidates. This process will help the committee narrow the pool and identify the most qualified candidates, a process we discuss in the next chapter.

---

*Authors' Note*: Sections of this chapter were taken from the following article: Hochel, S., & Wilson, C. E. (2006, Spring). Critically evaluating vitae: Tips on reading between the lines. *The Department Chair, 16*(4), 27–28.

# Chapter Six

# Identify Top Candidates

In Chapter 5, we discussed how to review and evaluate candidate materials. After all committee members have carefully reviewed the files, you need to meet to sort candidates into groups and identify your semi-finalists (the candidates you will contact for phone interviews). Then you need to plan for and conduct phone interviews with the semi-finalists and with their references. After this you are ready to select the finalists you will bring to campus. In this chapter, we offer suggestions for effectively and efficiently progressing through these important steps in hiring right.

## SELECT AND CONTACT THE SEMI-FINALISTS

There are several ways the committee can select the semi-finalists, and the choice will be influenced by the number of applicants and the size of the committee. An approach we find relatively quick and manageable is to sort candidates into the *yes, maybe,* and *no* groups. We start with areas of agreement because this can set a positive tone and establish a feeling of accomplishment. Once the committee has sorted those everyone agrees on, members discuss the remaining candidates.

The number in the *yes* group will vary with the position and the number of candidates. Usually the top group stands out from the rest and this determines the number of semi-finalists. If the list is reasonable in size (fewer than 10), all of the *yes* candidates can move ahead as semi-finalists. If the list is greater than 10, the committee should look more closely at the *yes* candidates and discuss each candidate's qualifications.

Once the semi-finalists have been identified, we prefer contacting them by email because of its efficiency. An email can convey the positive news and attend to business without wasting the time associated with playing phone tag. A sample email is shown in Appendix C.

We usually ask for 30–40 minutes for the interview, and we offer candidates a choice of days and times. We also ask permission to audiotape the phone interview for the sole purpose of allowing committee members unable to sit in on the interview to listen to it later. Some argue that audiotaping the interview can have an inhibiting effect. We have not found this to be the case. Sometimes committees may want to use videoconferencing for the interviews. We find the logistics to be difficult and the gains minimal.

## PREPARE AND CONDUCT PHONE INTERVIEWS WITH SEMI-FINALISTS

The interview with the applicant is no time for unplanned conversation: Too much is at stake to leave information gathering to chance. You need to do all you can to increase the chances of getting valid and helpful information. Toward that end, work as a committee to prepare for the interviews. We offer several tips, starting with developing an interview guide.

### Prepare a Structured Interview Guide

The guide consists of an opening, a series of logically organized and standardized questions to ask all applicants, questions unique to each candidate, and a plan for closing the interview. A well-prepared interview guide helps you stay on track and manage time, gives the interview a logical structure, ensures critical topics are covered, helps make certain all applicants are treated comparably, and makes note-taking easier. (We actually leave space between questions for note taking.) At the same time, the guide allows flexibility—for example, if you hear a comment that needs to be explored, you can deviate from the guide momentarily. (See Exhibit 6.1 for a sample guide.)

We will discuss the opening and closing of the interview later. Let's focus now on questions, beginning with an overview of some standard legal rules associated with a hiring inquiry.

*Review legal requirements.* In Chapter 2 we recommended that you begin the search process by having someone from HR or the legal office review the federal and state hiring regulations with you. Once you

---

EXHIBIT 6.1
_____

**Sample Interview Guide for the Phone Interview**

**(Search for Department Chair)**

**Candidate #_____ Name_____ Time_____**

*[Insert your plan for opening the interview here]*

1. What attracts you to this position at our institution?

   *[Leave space for note-taking after each question]*

   Let's begin by talking about the teaching part of the position.

2. Tell us some of the ways you work to create a classroom climate that is conducive to learning.

   Please describe one of your favorite or most innovative assignments for the introductory class and explain the educational rationale behind the assignment.

3. In your view, how can the teaching process best be evaluated?

   What have you learned from the student evaluations of teaching you have received?

   Staying on the subject of teaching evaluations, but moving into the administrative role of department chair:

   How would you deal with faculty members whose evaluations were below unit standards?

4. Please describe for us your most recent supervisory position and your style in that role.

   *[If candidate has not supervised faculty, skip 5A, ask 5B, and use alternate probes.]*

5. A. Supervising faculty can be challenging. Tell us about a time you supervised a faculty member who was difficult.
      *Probes:*
      - In what way was the person difficult?
      - How did you deal with him/her?
      - What was the resolution?
      - What would that person say about you as a supervisor?

   B. Hypothetical (substitute for 5A if the person has no supervisory experience): Supervising faculty can be challenging. Imagine that you supervise a faculty member who is missing office hours, doesn't turn in necessary paperwork in a timely fashion, comes late to department meetings, and about whom students complain. Tell us how you would handle this.

*continued*

*continued from previous page*

*Probes:*
- How would you deal with him/her?
- What kinds of things would you do or say?
- What would be your desired resolution?
- What if the situation did not improve?

6. In this day and age of scarce resources, it becomes every administrator's job to argue persuasively for your program. How in the past have you successfully convinced others of the worth of a unit or program?

7. We are a small program that has experienced a lot of growth. *[Give details.]* What ideas might you bring to the table to help us manage growth such that we can ensure high-quality experiences for students and faculty?

*Questions unique to each candidate.*

Let's shift gears. What questions would you like to ask us?

*[Insert your plan for closing the interview here]*

understand the laws, applying them to question writing and interviewing is not difficult. Remember these three rules:

- Base all questions on bona fide occupational qualifications (BFOQs).
- Ask no questions about protected characteristics such as religion, race, national origin, disability, and gender.
- Ask the same standardized questions of all candidates. (The difference between standardized questions and ones unique to each candidate is explained in this chapter.)

Following these rules in no way inhibits your ability to ask needed questions about job-related tasks. The following examples illustrate how you can phrase questions about two potentially sensitive topics.

Assume you are searching for an admissions counselor who will need to work one Sunday a month. Instead of asking candidates if their religion prohibits working on Sunday, simply ask if they can work one Sunday a month.

Assume you are hiring an office manager and the office needs to be open each day at 8:00 a.m. Instead of inquiring about candidates' child-care arrangements (a query usually posed only to women), ask: "The office needs to be open at 8:00 a.m. each day. Would you be able to be here at this time each weekday?"

The Americans with Disabilities Act and related EEO regulations specifically prohibit several areas of inquiry. For example, before hiring you may not ask about medical history; prior workers' compensation claims; past treatment for alcoholism, drug use, or mental illness; or work absenteeism due to illness (Weiss, 2004). If you follow the rule of asking only about BFOQs, your questions should be acceptable, as the following example illustrates.

> Assume you are hiring an assistant technical director for the theater. Instead of asking a candidate about a physical disability, ask about the specific job requirement. You could say: "The person holding this position has to assist in the construction of sets, move sets during productions, and be able to lift up to 40 pounds. Would you be able to do this?"

In this example, you would need to ask all candidates the question about set construction and lifting, not just those you know or suspect have a disability. Remember, you must treat all candidates equally.

Keep in mind that this overview is not an exhaustive examination of all pre-employment laws. Federal laws are complex, state laws vary, and all can change, so be sure to have a briefing with your HR department.

*Develop a set of standardized questions to ask each applicant.* You should have a set of job-related questions to ask each semi-finalist (including internal candidates) so you have a fair basis for comparison and stay on track. All the questions need to help you determine how qualified each candidate is for the position. This seems so obvious, we hesitate to say it. But we have both seen and read about interviewers asking questions that yield little or no useful information. One such question is "Tell us about yourself." Some candidates will give you useful information, but others may give you very long answers that tell you little or nothing.

Even when you have identified what you want to learn, writing effective questions is not all that easy. Questions that yield in-depth information about candidates' behaviors and attitudes are difficult to phrase, particularly on the spur of the moment, so questions should be written before an interview. To help avoid poorly written questions, we offer some don'ts. Don't ask questions that have obvious answers, such as

"How well do you work with others?" Don't ask questions that lead or suggest a preferred answer ("We are trying to expand our evening program. Would you be willing to teach in the evening?"). Don't ask overused questions for which candidates are likely to have prepared answers, such as "What do you see as your weaknesses?" Here are some do's: Use simple phrasing and straightforward language, know why you are asking the question, and rely primarily on questions about the applicants' past experiences.

The questions you prepare should be a mix of open and closed questions. When you need specific pieces of information, use closed questions that restrict the candidate's answer options ("What percentage of your time is spent dealing with students?"). When you want to give candidates the latitude to answer as they deem appropriate, use open questions ("What were some things about which you and your supervisor disagreed?"). A caution: If you ask too many closed questions, the applicant doesn't have the opportunity to open up and reveal the "real self." Your interview could also sound more like an interrogation.

Most of your questions should be behavioral questions that ask candidates to discuss past situations and how they handled them. Research indicates behavioral questions increase the validity of the selection interview because they elicit specific past behaviors of candidates and the best predictor of future performance is past performance (McDaniel, Whetzel, Schmidt, & Maurer, 1994). We might ask candidates for a development position, "Tell us about a time you successfully cultivated a relationship with a major donor." We learn about the candidate's ability to build a relationship, persuade and close a deal, and obtain good information for comparing applicants.

You may want a few situational or hypothetical questions asking candidates to put themselves into hypothetical situations. The idea here is that most people tend to act in real situations as they predict they will act in hypothetical ones. For example, we might ask a faculty candidate, "If in your first semester teaching here you discovered that more than half of your students were failing, what do you think you would do?" The key to writing situational questions is to make them specific and realistic but not overly complicated.

You may also want to ask some knowledge-based questions. For example, if interviewing for a library collections director, you may want to ask questions assessing candidates' knowledge of the publishing industry, the latest tools in digital libraries, and relevant information technology applications.

With any questions, and especially behavioral and situational questions, you must be prepared to probe. You many want to plan some probes, such as in this example: "Think back to a time when you had to deal with a difficult coworker. Tell us the situation and how you handled it." Possible probes are: "What happened next?" "What kind of reaction did you get?" "What was the long-term impact on your relationship?" and "If you had it all to do over again, what would you do differently?" Your goal in probing is to get complete answers so they can be compared.

Ideally, you should also create rating scales for each question, and interviewers should rate each answer rather than the entire interview to increase validity. The scales might be anchored with samples of excellent or poor answers marked by phrases that help interviewers consistently recognize an excellent answer, or might simply have a scale from 1 (poor) to 5 (excellent). We suspect that outside the research setting, most interviewers do not construct elaborate rating scales, and in fact, we have not used them in our searches. For more information on using rating scales, see Campion, Palmer, and Campion (1997).

We include a summary of tips for writing questions in Exhibit 6.2 and several sample questions in Exhibit 6.3. Obviously, you will need to

---

### EXHIBIT 6.2

#### Tips for Writing Questions

**Do**

- Have a set of standardized questions you ask of each candidate.
- Ask mostly behavioral questions.
- Know why you are asking each question.
- Ask only about BFOQs.
- Probe for full information.

**Don't**

- Ask questions with obvious answers.
- Ask leading questions.
- Ask overused questions.
- Ask too many closed questions.
- Ask for personal information.

EXHIBIT 6.3
_____

## Sample Interview Questions

### Quality of Past Work

- What do you think were some of your greatest accomplishments in your last job? Greatest disappointments or frustrations?
- In what ways did you contribute to the success of your unit at your last job?
- Tell me about a time when you needed outside help and had to ask someone for assistance. What was the situation? How did you decide whom to consult?
- We contact applicant's past employers. What do you think your past employers will say about your performance?
- Recall a time when you saw something that needed to be done in your organization and you stepped up and handled it.
- Recall a time when a coworker or supervisor criticized your work. What was the situation and how did you respond?

### Ability to Work Well with Others

- Tell me about your experience working on teams. (Probe for details because no one is going to say that they don't work well with others.)
- Tell us about a time when you helped out a colleague at work.
- When do you have difficulty communicating with others?
- Recall a time when you had to deal with a difficult coworker. What was the situation? How did you handle it? How was the relationship affected?
- What are some of the things you and your supervisor agreed about? Disagreed?
- How do you feel your supervisor could have done an even better job?

### Problem-Solving and Decision-Making Skills

- In your role as _____, what was the hardest decision you ever had to make?
- What are some things your department could do to be more success-ful? How would you go about implementing such improvements?

*continued*

*continued from previous page*

- Suppose you found that a student had plagiarized a small part of a final paper. What would you do?
- If you encountered this problem (describe a specific situation an employee might be expected to deal with), how would you handle it?
- If you could make one suggestion to higher administration at _____ University, what would it be?
- Describe a difficult problem that you had to resolve in your last job. How did you handle it? What did you learn from it?

### Ability to Set and Accomplish Goals

- If you could select an ideal working environment (or job), what would it be like? What are some things you would most want to avoid? Why?
- What would you look forward to in the future if you joined us? What additional education and training do you think you would need to reach your goals?
- Tell me about an innovation you introduced in your current workplace. What was it? How did you get the change made?
- What aspect of your work do you consider most crucial?
- How do you promote integrity in your unit/classroom?
- No one is perfect. Tell us about a time you changed your work behavior because of feedback you received from a coworker or boss.

### Ability to Manage Unit/Classroom

- How have you successfully motivated employees/students?
- How have you created a climate conducive to productivity/learning?
- How have you met the individual needs of subordinates/students?
- Tell us about a situation where your subordinates/students taught you an important lesson.
- Recall a program/course you designed. Describe step by step what you did and how it turned out.
- Tell us about a time when you had to talk with a subordinate whose work was below average. What were the circumstances? How did you deal with it? What was the result?

write questions based on the specific duties and qualifications for your position. We recommend avoiding questions about people's private lives, such as "What do you do to relax?" or "What are your hobbies?" These questions provide no information about work-related skills and abilities and could make you vulnerable to discrimination claims if information about protected characteristics (e.g., religion, age, ethnic origin) is obtained.

*Plan questions based on each candidate's file.* In addition to the set of standardized questions, you will also want to ask questions unique to each applicant. These questions should be based on the applicant's file and serve to clarify or expand on the information. For example, as we recommended earlier, ask candidates to give specifics in support of their statements of philosophy.

*Prepare the opening for the phone interview.* Make a plan for the opening to help ensure a smooth process, good use of time, and consistent treatment of all candidates. Keep conversation unrelated to the job (weather, sports events, etc.) to a minimum.

Start with introductions and verify that this is still a good time. Consider expressing appreciation for their application, and offering a compliment. This will help the candidate relax. Then let the person know what will happen in the ensuing time.

> Good morning. This is _____ from City University and I'm here with several members of the search committee. Is this still a good time to talk? Good. We were very impressed by your credentials so we've been looking forward to having this conversation. I'd like to verify that we have your permission to tape the interview (if you choose to tape). OK. In the next 30 minutes, we will be asking you a series of questions we have planned for each of our semi-finalists. I'll be asking the questions, but others may ask questions at the end. And before we finish, we'll give you the opportunity to ask us questions. If you're ready, let's get started.

We suggest starting with one or two questions the applicant can easily answer. This should further help your candidate relax.

*Prepare the closing for the interview.* The closing should summarize the interview, establish next steps, and end on a positive note. Be brief, as the following example illustrates.

Well, our time is about up. We appreciate your candid responses and your interest in our position. The committee will be meeting in the next two weeks to identify our finalists, and the committee chair will be in contact with you one way or another. It was nice talking with you.

## Work as a Team

The committee as a whole needs to agree on the standardized questions for the candidate interviews. Our approach is to have each committee member review the position duties, requirements, and performance criteria, write possible questions, and submit them to the chair so the chair can compile and distribute them. Then we meet to discuss, revise, and agree on the set of questions and the order of questions. Make sure the queries flow logically.

The number of questions needed varies depending on the types of questions and the time allotted for the phone interview. We typically have 9–12 questions for a 30- to 40-minute interview. Remember, you need time to probe. We recommend asking your most critical questions earlier in the interview, so if you need to skip any questions, you don't miss the most critical ones.

## Determine Your Interviewing Procedure

Have a clear procedure for conducting the phone interviews. Ideally, all committee members sit in on them, but this is usually impossible. Even when multiple people listen, we suggest you have one primary interviewer. Having one interviewer helps move the interview along briskly and assures the planned questions are asked in the time frame. Others should listen intently and ask any follow-up questions before inviting questions from the candidates. Committee members should anticipate what questions candidates might ask so they can be prepared to answer thoughtfully. If you do not tape the phone interviews, we suggest assigning one committee member to take notes to distribute to absent members.

## Review the Applicant's File Before the Interview

You need to know what is in the file and build on that information, not duplicate it. Having the file fresh in your mind will help you interpret information and ask probing questions.

## Interview Effectively

- Follow your interview guide, but be flexible. If a candidate provides information you think needs to be explored, pursue the information (but only if job-related). And if a question you planned to ask has been answered, skip it.
- Be conversational and avoid creating an atmosphere of interrogation.
- Listen attentively to what is said, how it is said, and what is left unsaid.
- Attend to nonverbal cues. For example, pay attention to long pauses, hesitations, and vocal variety.
- Probe for full answers to questions. You should use unplanned probes as needed, such as "Tell me more," or "Please, give me an example." The use of expressions of encouragement such as "uh huh," "humm," and "really" is also an effective way to motivate candidates to provide complete answers.
- Be comfortable with silence. Silence encourages a candidate to think and go beyond a canned answer.
- Be encouraging but neutral. Monitor your own reactions. For example, don't tell a candidate an answer was "perfect" or let your tone of voice convey displeasure with an answer.
- Interrupt only if a candidate is rambling.
- After asking planned questions, invite applicant questions. Candidates' questions may provide useful information about their desires and priorities.
- Make no promises about a candidate's standing in the selection process. Even if you think a candidate is abysmal or perfect, you can't be sure others will agree.

## Make Notes Right Away

Record impressions immediately after the interview. Even if you have a tape recording, technology can fail, plus you want to make notes about your overall perceptions of and reactions to the candidate. We recommend making notes on the interview guide (shown earlier in Exhibit 6.1).

## PREPARE AND CONDUCT PHONE
## INTERVIEWS WITH REFERENCES

Reference checks are vital to hiring good employees because these checks are often the only way to obtain information from a source other than the candidate. Search committee members often believe little is gained from checking references because of past experiences where perfunctory calls were only made to listed references. However, when done correctly, reference checks with listed and unlisted references can provide invaluable information that cannot be obtained any other way.

One other reason for conducting effective reference checks is to avoid charges of negligent hiring. Let's say you hire a professor who had pressured students for sexual favors at another institution and was fired as a result, and then the same behavior occurs at your institution. If you failed to check references or did not ask about disciplinary action or reprimands in your reference checking, then you may be vulnerable to a charge of negligent hiring. The key is whether the information was accessible to you and whether you should have known that a hire was unfit and had a previous, known problem. (For a discussion of the legal and ethical issues of getting and giving reference information, see Andler, 2003, and Stokes, 2000.) To obtain vital information, one question you should always ask a reference is whether the candidate's behavior was ever a cause for reprimand or disciplinary action.

We can't stress enough the need to contact unlisted references. So how do you locate appropriate people to contact? First, look in candidate files, as we suggest in Chapter 5, and identify any key people who did not write letters. For example, if you don't have a letter from a previous supervisor or coworker on a major project, contact them. Second, when interviewing any reference (listed and unlisted), ask them for names and contact information of people who have worked closely with the candidate. We have encountered several instances where references gave lukewarm and guarded recommendations, but freely gave the names of other people we could contact who were not hesitant to reveal significant problems. Third, consult a school or unit's web page for appropriate references. Even if you call people who are not in a good position to provide a reference, they will usually be able to give you other names. Our experience has taught us that by being persistent we can obtain honest, helpful information.

For all semi-finalists, conduct interviews with people who can provide you with helpful information. This includes:

- Listed references as needed to elucidate information in their letters or to obtain names of others you should contact
- At least two unlisted references (when you have obtained permission)
- At least one former or current supervisor
- Others as needed

Remember, you must treat all candidates comparably, so check references for internal candidates as well as external candidates.

We offer the following guidelines to help ensure you obtain the information needed to make high-quality hiring decisions.

### Obtain Written Permission to Check with Listed and Unlisted References

We recommend emailing all semi-finalists to 1) request permission to contact both listed and unlisted references, 2) ask for email addresses and phone numbers for listed references, and 3) inquire if there is anyone you should not contact and why. When candidates reply, you have their written permission for your records. Email responses are also quicker than the postal service. One strategy for controlling the committee's workload is to ask for this information when you set up phone interviews (see Appendix C).

Occasionally applicants may refuse your request to contact current supervisors and coworkers. We view this as acceptable as long as they give you permission to check references if they become finalists (let's say your top five). However, *we recommend against bringing a candidate to campus without first checking unlisted references*. We know of too many instances where a person was brought to campus and problems were immediately discovered, but the campus visit had to proceed, consuming much time, energy, and money, and damaging the reputation of those on the search committee. One of us vividly recalls a candidate who took such pains to avoid eye contact that he "talked to" the floor and potted plants for two very, very long days. In other instances, serious problems were discovered upon interviewing unlisted references *after* the campus visit.

## Review Your Previous Notes

When you evaluated the letters of recommendation, you completed the reference review sheet (see Exhibit 5.5 in the previous chapter) to make note of the strength of the letters, any red flags in the letters, and key areas for further exploration. You also identified people not listed by the applicant who are in a good position to provide information. After examining this form and reviewing the candidate evaluation form (see Exhibit 5.2 in the previous chapter), you should know whom to contact and the major topics to cover.

## Schedule Phone Interviews with References

Email references, introduce yourself and your task, request assistance, specify the time required for the phone interview (usually 20 minutes), and offer several possible appointment times. Ask them to let you know which time is convenient or offer alternatives. This helps avoid phone tag, and the references are less likely to be interrupted and more likely to take the time to thoroughly answer questions.

Given people's busy schedules, you might be tempted to email questions to references and ask them to respond, but resist this temptation. People are much less likely to be candid in writing than in a telephone conversation, and you cannot hear important nonverbal cues and probe as needed. Thus, never conduct the reference checks via email.

On rare occasion, a reference may refuse the request. If so, ask if institutional policy prohibits giving references. Regardless of the answer, contact appropriate others at the same institution to see if they will answer your questions. Although those in HR may only provide employment data, our experience calling dozens of unlisted references is that faculty, in particular, are willing to answer specific questions when told a candidate has given permission.

## Prepare a Guide for Interviewing References

This is similar to the guide prepared for the phone interviews with candidates. Along with the opening, closing, and standardized questions, you will want to prepare questions unique to each candidate based on the candidate's credentials and relationship to the reference.

Start by planning a few opening comments. Thank the reference and say that the candidate has provided written permission to talk to listed and unlisted references. Let the reference know if more than one person is participating in the interview. Then prepare easy-to-answer first questions such as, "What is your professional relationship to the candidate?" and "How long have your worked with the candidate?" Be sure you don't waste time asking questions already answered in the reference letter.

Now develop your set of standardized questions, keeping in mind EEO guidelines. Remember, you must ask the same core questions of all references to compare answers across candidates. Consider modifying the following questions to fit your position's requirements:

- Why is _____ looking for another position?
- Compare _____'s ability to work effectively with coworkers to others who have had similar responsibilities.
- What are _____'s most significant contributions to your unit?
- Consider recent meetings you have been in with _____. How would you describe him/her as a communicator?
- Which of _____'s qualities and characteristics will be hardest to replace in your department?
- How do you think _____'s performance could have been improved?
- Did _____'s conduct ever require any corrective action such as supervisory intervention, reprimands, or disciplinary action?

We recommend that you end the questions by asking the following:

- If you had the chance to rehire _____, what would be your hesitations?
- What else should our search committee know about _____'s professional performance and abilities?

When developing queries specific to each candidate, prepare questions to check the veracity of claims. As we've discussed, many people make their accomplishments look better on paper than they really are. For example, an applicant may claim primary responsibility for revising a department's curriculum when in actuality he or she rarely came to meetings and contributed little. Plan questions carefully because there is a right and wrong way to verify information. If you tell references what is on the candidate's vita and ask if this is correct, they are more likely to corroborate the information. Instead, say you know their department revised the curriculum and ask what role the candidate played. Ask open questions and do not provide the answer for the interviewee.

Be sure your questions are not in violation of EEO regulations. As previously discussed, EEO regulations do not prohibit asking about legitimate BFOQs, but you must take care when wording potentially sensitive items. Let's say you have a concern about a candidate's ability to speak acceptable English based on teaching evaluations and comments in reference letters. When interviewing a reference you cannot ask about a candidate's native language, which might reveal national origin. Instead, ask if the reference believes the candidate's English proficiency is sufficient to clearly communicate complex information to students or colleagues.

Finally, prepare a simple closing for the interview. If needed, ask for names and contact information for other possible references and then offer your thanks.

### Determine the Interview Procedure

As a general rule, two people should be assigned to conduct each reference call; yet we realize this may not always be feasible. Having two people is advantageous because you never know when damaging information may be disclosed or when different interpretations of a message may occur. Even when two people are assigned, we prefer having one primary interviewer, as in the phone interview with semi-finalists. The other should listen intently and have an opportunity at the end to ask questions.

You may be tempted to tape record interviews so all on the committee can hear them. Don't do it. References are much less likely to be candid if they know a conversation is being recorded.

### Make the Calls

At the appointed time, make your call and follow your interview guide, but be flexible when needed. Don't let an interview become perfunctory with your asking the expected questions and hearing the expected answers. If the reference provides information that needs to be clarified or pursued, do so, then return to your guide. For example, if you ask about a candidate's strengths, be sure to ask for specifics. If the reference isn't stretching the truth or being economical with it, he or she should be able to offer examples easily.

Give ample time for the reference to talk and avoid interrupting unless the interviewee is rambling or evading the question. Listen thoughtfully to answers and pay attention to what is not said. Also attend to nonverbal cues. Pay particular attention to hesitations that might suggest uncertainty about what to disclose.

If a reference begins to discuss illegal information such as age or marital status, politely interrupt and say, "Excuse me, but it is important that we focus only on job-related characteristics." Then rephrase your question.

During the interview, take careful notes and complete them immediately after ending the conversation. Remember that interviews with references should not be recorded, so the rest of the committee is counting on comprehensive notes. We leave space on the interview guide for note-taking. (See Exhibit 6.4 for a sample interview guide for references.)

## OBTAIN ADDITIONAL INFORMATION

Occasionally, the committee needs extra information and must go to additional sources. For example, information may need to be verified, such as school accreditation. If you have candidates who have not completed the required degree, you should verify the date for degree completion with the academic advisor.

In addition, we recommend conducting Internet searches on all top applicants. Within minutes you can uncover valuable information. In one search we heard about, committee members discovered a candidate's blog, which contained comments about students that committee members considered inappropriate and insensitive. The blog contributed to the committee's decision to reject the candidate. In another search, members discovered in newspaper articles that one candidate had been accused of sexual harassment. As a result, committee members were legally and ethically obligated to obtain more information. In this situation, members made additional calls and learned the charges were dropped with no evidence of wrongdoing. The information did not hurt the candidate; indeed, he was selected as a semi-finalist. In addition to "Googling" applicants, you should also check the social networking sites, such as facebook.com and myspace.com, to find personal blogs.

---

EXHIBIT 6.4
_____

### Structured Interview Guide for Reference Checking

**Reference Check for**_____ **Phone Interview with**_____ **(Listed/Unlisted)**

_[Insert your plan for opening the interview here]_

1. How long have you known _____? In what capacity?

   _[Leave space for note-taking after each question]_

2. How would you describe _____'s communication style?

3. How would you compare her/his performance with the performance of others who had similar responsibilities? (Probe for specifics if needed. Be sure that the reference discusses both teaching performance and collegiality if the reference is in a position to evaluate this.)

4. How would you evaluate this person on _____ (e.g., scholarly activities, supervisory effectiveness)?

5. Ask the following if not covered in the above questions.

   Please describe the strengths that you think _____ brought to your program.

   In what ways could _____ have improved his/her performance?

6. Did her/his conduct ever require any corrective action such as supervisory intervention or reprimands?

7. If you had a position similar to ours, would you recommend that he/she be strongly considered?

8. What should we consider regarding _____ that we have not asked about?

_[Insert your plan for closing the interview here]_

Interviewer's notes:

---

## EVALUATE THE REFERENCE AND INTERNET INFORMATION

When reviewing the information obtained from your reference checks and Internet searches, remember that everyone has strengths and weaknesses, so uncovering negative information is certainly not a reason for rejection. If you get negative information, ask:

- How salient is the information to the essential job qualifications?
- Is the candidate otherwise strong?

- Is the source credible?
- Have we verified the information?

Be fair to candidates. Any person who has had to make difficult decisions affecting others may have earned the enmity of some. So check
information with a variety of sources.

## SELECT FINALISTS FOR CAMPUS VISITS

At this point, the committee must evaluate each semi-finalist and decide
whom to invite to campus as finalists. Many times, a top group of candidates emerges after discussion, but if this is not the case, we recommend individuals rank order each semi-finalist. Then the group averages
the rankings to determine the top group. Those who are not selected as
finalists should be placed into the *maybe* or *no* groups, as appropriate.

During discussions, major disagreements may occur, or you may
have to deal with a difficult committee member. When problems arise in
groups, we often look to the committee chair for resolution, but effective
group efforts are the responsibility of all members of the committee. You
can help avoid unpleasant confrontations and defuse tension by taking
ownership of your opinions. Do this by using "I language," such as saying, "I don't think he is a top candidate because . . ." or "I'm in favor of
this candidate because . . ." You can also help the committee by making
sure discussion stays focused on the qualifications required for success. If
a committee member becomes contentious, do not respond in kind. Go
back to the requirements of the position and each candidate's qualifications. And as discussed previously, use the democratic method: When no
new information is contributed and the same points are being repeated,
vote.

After selecting the finalists, we recommend the committee examine
candidates in the *maybe* group. If you are fortunate to have several well-
qualified candidates in this group, consider holding the strongest in
reserve. If your initial hiring efforts are unsuccessful, you can return to
this group.

## COMMUNICATE WITH CANDIDATES

So far in the process we have recommended communicating with candidates via email. Now is the time we prefer to contact candidates by

phone. The number of candidates is more manageable, and the need for personal conversation is greater. Finalists may have questions, you may need to broach the subject of salary and benefits, and you may need to begin planning the campus visit. For consistency, these calls should all come from the same person, usually the committee chair.

Notify applicants who are no longer in contention for the position by mail as soon as possible. A kind rejection letter is sometimes hard to write; keep it simple and remember to do what you can to maintain a positive image for your unit and your institution. We show sample rejection letters in Appendix B.

Candidates in the reserve group also need to be notified by mail at this time: Do not keep them in the dark. We recommend openly telling them they are in the reserve group. Let them know the search process is moving forward, but their applications are still considered open. A sample of this type of letter is shown in Appendix B.

## CONCLUSION

The task of identifying your top candidates is difficult yet manageable. By working as a team to select the semi-finalists and going through the steps necessary to identify the finalists, the search committee is well positioned to do an excellent job when finalists come for the campus visit, which we discuss in the next chapter.

*Authors' Note:* Sections of this chapter were taken from the following article: Hochel, S., & Wilson, C. E. (2006, Winter). Checking references: A vital step in employee selection. *The Department Chair, 16*(3), 14–16.

# Chapter Seven

## Arrange and Host the Campus Visits

You have exerted great effort to get to this point, but your work is not complete. You need to plan and host the campus visits, which have at least two purposes. First, they are a means to continue gathering as much good quality information as possible. Second, they give your unit and institution a chance to "show its stuff" and persuade candidates that the position is right for them. In this chapter, we discuss ways to ensure that the campus visits effectively meet these two purposes.

### UNDERSTAND THE CHALLENGE

The tasks you face at this point may seem daunting. The finalists you bring to campus will make concerted efforts to influence you positively about hiring them. Most people from the dominant U.S. culture have read or been coached about how to interview effectively. They know to be well-groomed, professionally attired, and nonverbally engaged. The Internet is replete with career coaching sites promising to teach job seekers how to ace an interview. The author of "the best selling job-hunting book in the world" tells job hunters to "Decide what image you're going to try to convey" (Bolles, 2001, p. 199). Some candidates are highly effective at this image management process; however, these candidates may not be the most qualified or the best suited for the job. Likewise, some candidates are less effective at image management. They are not as articulate and polished under pressure, but in fact may be the most qualified for the position. So you must make choices that help lead to sound, valid decisions.

## USE MULTIPLE METHODS OF
## INFORMATION GATHERING

To increase the predictive validity of your selection process, we propose using a variety of information gathering methods. Some methods are traditional (interviews and presentations) and some are not so traditional (critiquing student work, role-playing, demonstrating specialized knowledge). We realize committees may hesitate to use some of these nontraditional methods for fear of offending candidates or creating an unpleasant interview experience for them. Finalists for faculty and high-level administrative positions are not usually accustomed to being "tested" during a campus visit. Yet we believe highly qualified candidates will not be offended when asked to write a critique or engage in a role-play, and in fact may be impressed by your commitment to hiring right. Of course, you must select methods that are clearly tied to job duties and position requirements, apply them equally to all candidates, and conduct them in a respectful, nonthreatening way that conveys your seriousness about finding the right person for the position.

### Use Traditional Methods

*Interviews.* This is the most common method of information gathering, even though early research indicated the interview had low predictive validity (Arvey & Campion, 1982). Fortunately, recent studies are much more positive about the possible validity of the interview as a selection tool (Salgado & Moscoso, 2002). We use the word *possible* because certain conditions must be met or interviews will be poor predictors of job performance (Schmidt & Hunter, 1998). First, research indicates validity is improved by asking all candidates well-prepared questions based on a thorough job analysis (Campion, Palmer, & Campion, 1997). Second, for interviews to be valid predictors, they need to be structured (McDaniel, Whetzel, Schmidt, & Maurer, 1994). (Structured interviews were discussed in more detail in Chapter 6.) Campion et al. write: "In the 80-year history of published research on employment interviewing . . . few conclusions have been more widely supported than the idea that structuring the interview enhances reliability and validity" (p. 655).

To prepare a structured interview, you need to develop an interview guide consisting of a set of carefully planned questions to ask of all applicants plus questions unique to each candidate, as you did for the phone interview. (See Chapter 6 for a discussion of the components of the guide and sample standardized questions.) Even though you are using a structured interview, realize this format is not inflexible—there is latitude for probing and for skipping questions a candidate has already answered. Huffcutt and Arthur (1994) found that some amount of flexibility did not significantly reduce the overall validity of the structured interview.

In our experience, it is impossible that all interviews during an extended campus visit will be structured ones, but there should be several structured interviews during the visit. Whether using structured or unstructured interviews, you will get better information and avoid problems—including being swayed by well-delivered BS—if you don't fall victim to the following common interviewing mistakes:

- *Talking too much.* As a general rule, you should only talk 20% of the time and the candidate 80% (Kirkwood & Ralston, 1999). Unfortunately the percentages are frequently reversed.
- *Not taking notes.* You can't remember all that was said, and note-taking requires interviewers to be attentive. Taking notes also helps interviewers avoid giving preference to the first and last interviewees (recency and primacy effects) (Campion et al., 1997) and helps resolve disagreements over what a candidate said.
- *Not preparing questions.* You can't expect to come up with well-phrased, lawful questions on the spur of the moment.
- *Signaling the preferred answers.* You can do this verbally or nonverbally. Let's assume a candidate is telling you how her department could be improved and your nonverbals indicate you think her ideas are absurd. If she is astute, she will notice, adjust her ideas, and be less candid in other answers. You want to look interested, but you don't want to telegraph your opinion.
- *Not probing enough.* You should frequently use questions like "Could you give me an example?" or "Tell me more."
- *Just having a chat.* We have heard some faculty say they can "size up" a candidate best by chatting informally with them. They are deluding themselves.

Nothing has 100% predictive validity, which is the ability to predict future job performance and satisfaction with 100% certainty. But you can increase your ability to make a valid decision by using structured inter-

EXHIBIT 7.1
_____

**Increasing the Predictive Validity of Interviews**

- Ask well-prepared questions based on a job analysis.
- Use structured interviews.
- Avoid common interviewing mistakes.

views, writing questions based on needs identified in the position analysis, and avoiding common interview mistakes.

*Presentations/question-and-answer sessions.* Effective oral presentation skills are a criterion for most positions, so consider having finalists give an oral presentation with a question-and-answer time. Candidates for faculty positions are frequently asked to teach a class or discuss their research, and candidates for many other positions should also give a presentation. Regardless of the position, follow these guidelines:

- Be sure all candidates have a comparable presentation assignment.
- Make the assignment and audience as realistic as possible (e.g., have faculty candidates teach an actual class; have instructional technology candidates teach a web page design workshop to faculty and staff).
- Be certain you clearly communicate to the candidate who will be in the audience. You hope candidates will change their approach depending on whether the audience consists of mostly students, faculty, or staff.
- Immediately after the presentation has ended, solicit feedback from all participants. A sample feedback form for a classroom presentation is shown in Exhibit 7.2.

## Use Less Traditional Methods

*Critique student/subordinate work.* One way to gather information about the job skills of candidates is to have them critique a student's or subordinate's work. For example, you could have all candidates for director of admissions critique a subordinate's recruitment campaign, candidates for a computer graphics position could evaluate student projects, and candidates for an English composition position could grade a short student essay. You aren't doing this to see if the candidates evaluate the way you

---

EXHIBIT 7.2

**Evaluation of Classroom Presentation**
**Candidate for Assistant Professor**

### Candidate's Name

Members of the search committee want your feedback. Please complete and drop into the box at the front of the room before leaving. Thank you.

Was the material in the lecture:

- Clear?
- Organized?
- Effectively delivered?
- Of an appropriate depth for a college-level class?

Did the presentation:

- Keep your interest?
- Add to your knowledge?

Based on this presentation, would you like to take a class from this instructor? What other comments do you have for us?

---

do. Rather, you are assessing the insight, knowledge, communication skills, and standards of the candidates.

*Demonstrate specialized knowledge.* Ads frequently specify that a school is seeking a candidate with specialized knowledge, such as web-based recruitment and admissions systems, Internet development languages, desktop publishing programs, and accreditation guidelines. You may want to ask a few questions or design a simple test having *all* candidates demonstrate the needed proficiency.

*Participate in role-plays.* In a role-play, candidates are asked to interact with another person as if they already have the job. Role-playing isn't for every position, and some people are not comfortable with it. But when appropriate and used well, it can provide much useful information about job skills. For example, if hiring a director of housing, set up a situation where a person role-plays a student who is angry about a roommate situation and is demanding a move. If hiring a director of advancement, you could role-play a meeting with a potential donor. When arranging the role-play, follow these guidelines:

- When writing the role-play situation, make it realistic without making it too simple or too complex.
- Select a colleague to do the role-play whose judgment you trust and who will be comfortable with the part.
- Don't have observers: They make the situation too awkward and unrealistic.
- Be sure your colleague knows what you are looking for in the candidate's behavior.
- Immediately after the role-play, get the colleague's feedback about the candidate's performance so you can share this with the committee.
- Have the same colleague do the same role-play with all the finalists.

*Respond to a case/situation.* Similar to a role-play, candidates are asked to respond to a realistic situation, but here they respond in writing. You may find it helpful to review the performance criteria to see if you have adequately assessed all the major skills and requirements. If not, responding to a case may be a helpful option. For example, assessing ethics is very difficult—it does no good to ask someone about their ethics. But you can ask candidates to respond to a case where they have to make ethical choices, such as having candidates for a public relations position react to a case about dealing with a reporter probing for information about an embarrassing organizational incident. The responses could give you information about candidates' problem-solving, decision-making, and critical thinking skills, as well as their ethics.

The case is also a good way to assess candidates' writing abilities in a way that is not offensive. Most ads we see identify writing ability as a job criterion. And while you can assess a candidate's writing in the file, relying totally on submitted materials can be dangerous. A colleague at another school told us about hiring a bookstore manager whose first memo to the entire campus would have received an F in any English 101 class. The members of the search committee were embarrassed and concluded someone else must have helped him prepare his file. To avoid this kind of embarrassment without seeming inappropriate, you might have finalists write or respond to a letter or email. For example, you could have finalists for a student activities director write a short response to a student complaint about an event on campus. If you choose to have candidates respond to a case or a situation, keep the following in mind:

- Write a situation that is realistic for the position and institution.
- Provide candidates with enough detail to respond effectively.
- Give candidates difficult choices or multiple interpretations with no obvious solution.
- Make sure directions are clear, and if you are asking candidates to respond to questions, be sure they are open-ended and understandable.
- Give candidates ample time to respond.
- Determine in advance how you will evaluate the response.

*Other.* Think about the position, duties, and job criteria, and then be creative in exploring other methods of gathering information. For example, if interviewing for a bookstore manager, you could give finalists time to walk around the facility and make observations. Then ask them specific questions about their opinions and ideas for change. If hiring for positions in alumni relations or advancement, you could plan a social event or meeting and observe the candidates as they interact with different constituents.

## PLAN FOR AND HOST THE VISITS

Now that you know what methods you will use to gather additional information about your candidates, you can begin arranging the campus visits.

### Decide Whom to Involve and How

*Determine whom.* Chapter 2 discussed how to identify your constituent groups and involve representatives in ways other than committee membership. Revisit this information as you make choices about hosting campus visits, keeping in mind the position, length of the visit, and campus norms. Recognize that you involve others to get their assessments of the candidates, see how candidates interact with others, allow candidates to meet with key groups and individuals, and help ease the transition of the successful candidate. Accordingly, consider including the hiring unit, the head of that unit, the dean or other higher level administrator, members of interfacing units, and a representative from HR. Be sure to schedule time for candidates to meet with the person handling the reimbursement of expenses so all the necessary forms are completed and signed. Remember also that not all higher level administrators need to meet with candidates, but consider the message sent when making choices. If candidates for a faculty position do not meet with the dean, the message sent may be one of inaccessibility, which may dissuade candidates from wanting the job.

Unfortunately most units have members who are "difficult." Perhaps in your unit there is a person who has a grudge against the administration and consequently has nothing good to say about the unit or the institution. Perhaps you have a coworker who is a perpetual rule breaker who cannot be trusted to adhere to EEO guidelines during the search. Difficult coworkers can undermine the success of your search, so you want to think through their involvement carefully. One option is not to include these difficult colleagues at all; however, that is not always a possible choice. We recommend you try to limit the time candidates spend with the difficult employee, and if possible, schedule the difficult person only for group time or have colleagues meet with candidates in pairs. Avoid including the difficult individual in unstructured sessions with candidates, like lunches or social hours. And if you learn that a colleague has ignored EEO guidelines, notify your HR representative and remove the violator from the process.

*Decide how.* After determining who needs to be involved, decide how to involve them. Some people need to have one-on-one interviews with candidates, but others could just attend a presentation or meeting, dine with the candidate, or attend a social hour. An alumnus or student employee could give a tour of the campus, and a community member with strong ties to your unit could provide a tour of the surrounding area.

Questions often arise about having one-on-one interviews or panel interviews with candidates. The research on panel interviews is not extensive, but Herriott (2003) reports that panel interviews provide little gain in predictive validity. Other benefits may accrue, however. Group members see how the candidate interacts with a group, everyone hears the same responses, and the amount of time used is reduced. Also, people are generally more accepting of decisions they had a role in making. Further, a panel interview is often the only realistic option for having the candidate interact with a group (e.g., students, alumni). A mix of both individual and panel interviews may be most effective.

If you do use a panel interview, create a plan so group members ask each candidate the same key questions (e.g., provide students with a list of appropriate questions and encourage each to select one or two to ask). After the meeting, get feedback from the group members. We ask attendees to provide a written evaluation of the candidate's strengths, weaknesses, and overall suitability. However, if you prefer a group evaluation of the candidate, assign a leader to keep discussion focused on job requirements and ensure that all members express their opinions. A vocal minority should not be allowed to sway the group's opinion, nor should those with more power or authority be allowed to dictate the group's recommendation.

### Prepare (and Share) the Itinerary

Consider the following as you plan the itinerary.

*Consult first with those who have the most inflexible schedules.* If you know the meeting with the provost is usually the most difficult to schedule, begin with this appointment.

*Check with candidates about special requests.* They may want time to meet with the grants officer on campus or talk to a realtor. They may have special dietary needs.

*Be realistic.* Only so much can be squeezed into a campus visit, so make deliberate choices about whom to involve and how much time to allocate. For instance, if you know the dean has routinely taken twice the allotted time to interview previous candidates, then allow more time or talk to the dean about the schedule. Build in some catch-up time in case the schedule gets behind.

*Vary the schedule.* Back-to-back interviews can be exhausting, so mix up the type of meetings you schedule to avoid tiring candidates excessively.

*Allow the candidates some free time.* They may want to review notes for a presentation, check out holdings in the library, or just walk around campus.

*Have escorts.* Carefully select people to transport candidates to and from the airport, hotel, and campus. Choose people who will make a positive impression and convey your commitment to hiring right. Arrange for escorts to walk candidates from one meeting to the next. In addition to being useful to candidates, these escorts help you stay on schedule because their arrival signifies that an appointment time is over.

*List names and titles of everyone involved on the itinerary.* This information is valuable to candidates.

*Schedule a wrap-up meeting.* Toward the end of the visit, be sure to have a meeting with the committee or the committee chair to give people an opportunity to ask any final questions. This also provides needed closure to the visit.

*Send out a draft itinerary.* If there are any problems, you want to know about them ahead of time.

*Send the final itinerary to the candidate and all involved parties.* But be ready for last minute changes.

### Prepare the Campus Participants

Candidate meetings should not be scheduled without preparing the participants. Provide anyone who will meet with the candidates three pieces of information: 1) a copy of the position announcement, 2) the candidate's credentials (provide access to the file or prepare a short summary) and 3) a copy of the university's EEO guidelines. When disseminating this information, stress the importance of reading and following the EEO guidelines. For groups and individuals who will interview the candidates (and not just attend a social gathering), you must emphasize the importance of planning job-related questions to ask of each candidate following a structured format.

One way to increase the predictive validity of your interviews is to ask a large number of questions on different topics (Campion et al., 1997). Too often, candidates are asked the same question ("Tell me why you want to work here") in interview after interview. Committee members should agree to cover different areas in their interviews to allow more topics to be addressed. This should also keep the interviews more interesting for candidates, avoid the perception that you are disorganized, and provide candidates with a realistic idea of the different requirements for the job.

Campus representatives must also be prepared to deal with potentially awkward situations. If an institution has funding difficulties or a department has significant problems, those knowledgeable about the situation must be prepared to answer questions honestly. Give candidates enough information to provide a realistic picture of the challenges they will face if they are offered and accept the position. We recommend assigning one or two people to raise any significant issues so candidates are informed but not overwhelmed by negativity.

### Woo the Candidates

As stated earlier, you cannot forget that candidates are evaluating you, so you must deliberately work to convince top candidates of the desirability of your position and institution. What can you do?

*Provide information in advance.* Before a top candidate comes for the campus visit, send a packet of information from the institution and the local Chamber of Commerce. Include a recent student newspaper, the campus magazine, newsletters, and the current catalogue. Visit the chamber to get information on the community. Candidates may be concerned about job opportunities for a spouse; they may want to know about housing, schools, shopping, and cultural opportunities.

*Give candidates sufficient opportunities to ask questions.* In addition to providing desired information, the opportunity to ask questions helps candidates feel positive about the interview experience (Gilliland & Steiner, 1999).

*Communicate needed information.* Ensure that topics important to the candidate are discussed. For example, an appropriate administrator should discuss the evaluation process used on campus, as well as salary and benefits. Other issues of import include the reason the position is open, the financial stability of the department and institution, plans for growth, and funds for professional development.

*Be honest.* Don't set up a new employee for disappointment. Changing jobs is hard enough without finding out one was misled. This means you must be ready to candidly discuss problems. For example, if a department has a serious rift, discuss it in factual terms, and tell candidates how the problem is being handled.

*Don't make the visit more stressful than necessary.* Ralston and Brady (1994) found candidates' satisfaction with interview communication strongly influenced their employment decisions, more than previous research had indicated, in fact. Keep this in mind as you plan the itinerary. For example, use panel interviews judiciously since they are perceived as more stressful than one-on-one interviews.

*Make the process transparent.* Throughout the day, let candidates know what is happening and why. This ranges from providing a rationale for the role-playing experience to explaining why the itinerary has a last-minute change.

*Show off your stuff.* Candidates are obviously evaluating the work environment of your institution, and you should highlight positive aspects. For example, if new hires get brand-new computers or new office furniture, tell them.

*Communicate the next steps.* Let the candidates know the time frame for a decision and any other actions the committee will take. Abide by the time frame or let candidates know if you have a delay.

No matter how the search turns out, you want all candidates to leave your campus with a positive impression. They will tell others about the experience, you may have a later opening they could effectively fill, and they may have children that someday they will send to college. Your reputation should remain positive, even if you don't extend a candidate an offer.

## CONCLUSION

The campus visits are a critical component of hiring right. Be mindful of the benefits of using multiple methods of information gathering and make thoughtful decisions about what methods to use, whom to involve, and how. As you plan for and host the campus visits, be sure to consider our strategies for persuading candidates to think positively about your unit and institution. By following these suggestions, you can create a positive image with candidates while also gathering good quality information for making a fair and defensible decision.

# Chapter Eight

# Close the Deal

Some authors compare the task of a search committee to that of a detective who has to examine records, gather data, and scrutinize information carefully to make a well-reasoned decision. Certainly similarities exist. As with the detective, your task is sometimes made easy when you discover a "smoking gun" that disqualifies a candidate (e.g., the candidate's presentation is dreadful, or responses to student questions are downright rude, or the purported expert on accreditation can't answer even basic questions on the topic). More often, though, your task is not so easy: You must analyze, deduce, gather more evidence, and agonize before making a decision. You have some hard work to do as you evaluate all the information you have gathered to make your hiring recommendation.

## AVOID SERIOUS PITFALLS

Too often, committees do excellent work up to the point of deliberations and then they fall victim to mistakes that can have long-term negative consequences. Don't succumb to the following major hiring errors:

- *Don't rush to make the final decision.* You are tired, have a hundred other things to do, and want the search to be over. But if you need clarification or additional information, the time spent making calls is time well spent.
- *Don't settle.* If you make a bad hire, you can be stuck with the person for years. No one wants to conduct a new search after spending all the time and effort on one. Not hiring is disappointing and

frustrating, but selecting the best out of a pool of weak candidates will cause serious problems in the long run.

- *Don't give in to pressure.* Your supervisor may want the position filled, but you have to "live" with the hire on a daily basis.
- *Don't hire on intuition.* If a candidate "just feels right" but you can't articulate your reasons, then something is wrong.
- *Don't ignore gut feelings.* This may seem contradictory to "don't hire on intuition," but it isn't. It simply means you need to closely examine the reasons for your reactions and then articulate your rationale.
- *Don't fall victim to the halo effect.* If you like one thing about a candidate, you may be inclined to assume you will like other things and not examine the candidate's other credentials and behaviors as closely.
- *Don't be overly influenced by a negative.* Every candidate has negatives, and if you let one negative lead to an overall negative evaluation, you may overlook a good hire.

## REVIEW THE LOGISTICS

Prior to the deliberation meeting, committee members should read all the feedback forms completed by others during the campus visit and bring all the evaluation forms they completed for each candidate to the meeting. Plan for a long meeting. At the beginning, the chair should review the committee's charge, the job requirements and performance criteria, and the importance of confidentiality of the deliberations. During the meeting, evaluate all candidates invited to campus—even those no one liked—because this will help you prepare the report to the hiring authority. Appoint a scribe to record the committee's assessment of each candidate. If one or all candidates have unanimous support, your task is easier. But if not, we recommend voting by secret ballot so members have more confidence that their votes will stay private and not cause relationship problems with the new hire.

## CONSIDER THE BASIS FOR MAKING YOUR DECISION

### Assess Candidates Based on BFOQs

Earlier, you spent significant time analyzing the position and carefully crafting a position announcement to communicate clearly the position requirements and performance criteria. To make the best possible decision, you must make your final recommendations based on these requirements and criteria. We recommend reviewing your position analysis and evaluation form so committee members are reminded to stay focused on the critical BFOQs. Keeping the committee's focus on the requirements and performance criteria helps ensure that deliberations are based only on BFOQs. For instance, one committee member may really like one candidate—she just felt a connection—but a review of the qualifications may help her realize the person isn't the best match for the position. Or during the deliberations one member may argue a candidate is "too good" and won't stay at your school. If the qualifications are front and center, you can more easily point out this assumption is unfair and certainly not a BFOQ. (And doesn't your college want to hire the best?)

## Guard Against Perceptual Biases

Even with the best effort to stay focused on BFOQs, perceptual biases are inevitable and can creep into decision processes. We all want to believe we don't judge people on characteristics like appearance, but the research proves otherwise. And while EEO laws protect candidates from several significant areas of prejudice, including race, sex, and religion, laws do not protect candidates from other unfair prejudices and biases. Your best defense is to recognize biases and guard against them. Accordingly, we discuss biases based on physical appearance and voice because they are common and often unconscious and can lead to unfair and indefensible decisions.

*Bias against unattractive people.* Much research suggests that physically attractive applicants are more likely to get a job over unattractive ones, if other qualifications are equal (Knapp & Hall, 2006; Marlowe, Schneider, & Nelson, 1996). After reviewing available research, Ilkka (1995) discovered that "attractive males and females are viewed as more sociable, friendly, competent, self-confident, popular, and more likely to succeed, as well as being better adjusted than people judged to be unattractive" (p. 4).

*Bias against the obese.* After reviewing relevant literature, Roehling (1999) concluded, "A substantial body of research suggests that bias against overweight individuals is pervasive in Western cultures. Overweight people are frequently stereotyped as emotionally impaired, socially handicapped, and as possessing negative personality traits" (p. 969). As Roehling discusses, this bias extends to the hiring decision.

*Bias against short men.* Several studies suggest that short men are not perceived as competent and are victims of discrimination in the job market (Knapp & Hall, 2006).

*Bias against certain accents.* Based on speakers' accents, people make judgments about their intelligence, personality, and other traits. For example, in one study Hispanic English speakers were rated low in comparison to other speakers on success, ability, and social awareness (Knapp & Hall, 2002). People are frequently unaware of the many judgments they make based on accents. For example, an interviewer may believe that someone with an upper-class British accent is more dependable than someone with a Jamaican accent, or that someone with a Bostonian accent is more intelligent than someone with a southern accent.

*Bias against "vocally unattractive" voices.* Much research indicates we stereotype individuals based on how they sound. For instance, a person with a squeaky, high-pitched voice is perceived as having different personality traits and attitudes than someone with a resonant, lower-pitched voice. Research also suggests we tend to see vocally attractive people as more socially skilled than those with unattractive voices (Semic, 1999).

Many other biases exist, such as ones for or against certain colleges or for or against certain research areas. Biases are serious concerns because often we don't recognize how they affect our perception. For example, let's say a candidate for dean is particularly attractive and has an "upper-class" Bostonian accent. The candidate looks and sounds like many people's perception of a dean. As a result, some interviewers may not recognize vague answers and fail to follow-up as they would with other candidates.

Let us reiterate. Fair, defensible decisions that result in hiring the best candidate for the position require that you stay focused on position requirements and performance criteria (BFOQs).

## EVALUATE CANDIDATE INFORMATION

### Review All the Information

As you evaluate your candidates, be sure to look at *all* the information you have obtained. Don't rely only on the information from the campus visit. If you rely solely on the campus visit, you may hire the candidate who is a master interviewee—someone skilled in BS who knows what to say and how to say it. When you interview candidates for a day, you have only a small sampling of behavior, and you don't know if the sample is biased or representative. We hope what we see is what we'll get, but it only takes one bad hire to learn this is not always the case.

To increase the validity of your decision, you must evaluate the information obtained in the campus visit along with the information from the candidate's submitted materials and the comments of listed and unlisted references. Let's say Candidate A gave a stellar lecture when on campus and Candidate B gave a satisfactory performance. Candidate A has three years of average teaching evaluations while Candidate B has three years of outstanding evaluations. In this case, the combined evidence suggests Candidate B is the better teacher. Again, don't look only at the campus visit. Look at the total package.

## Consider the Strength of the Evidence

As you assess each candidate's suitability, decide how confident you are with your evidence.

*Is the evidence compelling?* Did the candidate and references provide you with convincing details that make you confident in your decision? What behaviors from the candidate's past indicate he or she can be an effective performer in the future? The committee should look for concrete examples and descriptive language rather than more general and evaluative language.

*How consistent is the information?* For evidence to be considered strong, you should find consistency in what the candidate said, what the references told you, and what you and others observed. Consistent information is more reliable and thus more valid. When information is inconsistent, consider the nature, source, and extent of the inconsistency.

## Follow a Systematic Procedure

When you deliberate, do not begin by making global judgments about each candidate's suitability. If you go immediately to a global assessment, you increase the chances of overlooking some performance criteria, treating candidates unevenly, making biased decisions, and having more contentious discussions. In addition, when you make global assessments, you may overlook red flags or information gaps that need to be addressed.

Rather, begin by answering the following question for each candidate: How well does this candidate meet each performance criterion? For example, refer to the evaluation form presented in Chapter 5 (Exhibit

5.2). The form lists position requisites and performance criteria such as senior level experience, collaborative leadership style, and rapport with students. Candidates who did not meet the requisites would not have been invited to campus, so the search committee for this position now needs to consider the candidates' effectiveness for each criterion from senior level experience to rapport with students.

After the committee has assessed each candidate's ability to perform in each area, members should answer four additional questions that should lead to a fair and defensible evaluation of each candidate:

- What are the candidate's strengths?
- What are the candidate's weaknesses?
- What does the candidate bring to the unit and/or institution?
- What do we need that the candidate does not bring?

When evaluating candidates, consistency is crucial. Consider again the evaluation form in Exhibit 5.2. If the standard for excellence on collaborative leadership style is set higher for an African-American candidate than a Caucasian candidate, then the committee may be letting prejudice influence its judgment. Likewise, if the committee considers rapport with students a critical factor for a female candidate but not for a male, then bias may be unconsciously operating.

Finally, have minimum acceptable standards in mind, so you are comparing candidates to a desired level of competency in each area rather than comparing candidates to one another. If candidates are compared to one another, and they are all relatively weak, you can end up making a bad hire.

### Gather More Information as Needed

Frequently a committee decides it needs more information to make a good decision. Usually this involves contacting additional references to obtain specific information or confirm impressions made during the campus visits. For example, in a search for chancellor we served on, some on the committee were impressed with one candidate while others had serious reservations based on the candidate's poor interactions with students. After the visit, the committee chair contacted the student activities director and student government president at the candidate's current institution and asked specific questions about the candidate's past interactions with students and student perceptions of the candidate. When you do need more information, decide as a committee who should be contacted and by whom. The more personal the contact with a reference, the more likely you are to get honest information. For example, if someone you know and trust worked at the same college as the candidate, then ask this person to make a few reference calls.

### Decide on Your Recommendation

If you have a strong candidate and feel confident in the validity of the evidence, then the decision to make a hiring recommendation is easy. If no strong candidate exists, then discuss alternatives. Do you have time to reopen the search? Do you have qualified candidates held in reserve? Can you cover the job duties in another way and wait to advertise again at a later date?

A failed search happens for many reasons; some are under the control of the committee and some are not. When a search fails, the committee should meet to explore the likely reasons for this (e.g., late advertising, limited recruitment, unrealistic job responsibilities, low salary). Then the chair should discuss these reasons with the hiring authority before a new search begins.

In the earlier section on pitfalls, we discussed the importance of "not settling" by picking the best out of a pool of weak candidates. However, it is easy for this to happen—committee members are tired and frustrated and may talk themselves into thinking the candidate will be better when on campus or when trained and adjusted to a new environment. They may rationalize they can't do any better if they wait. If you have these thoughts, just think of one incompetent or hostile employee on campus and consider the damage done by this one individual. If excellence is your goal, do not settle.

## FINISH THE JOB

### Defend the Decision

Whether your decision is not to hire because there is no strong candidate or whether you recommend one or more candidates to the hiring authority, you need to prepare a persuasive defense of your recommendation. This should not be difficult since you conducted the position analysis, identified the job qualifications, completed forms recording your evaluation of information provided by references and candidates, and analyzed candidates based on BFOQs. The defense frequently takes the form of a discussion of perceived strengths and weaknesses followed by an overall assessment of what a candidate will bring to the institution. If negotiations are needed to attract a candidate, the more compelling your arguments are, the better.

## Do Final Verifications

If you have not already checked your finalists' degrees (or at least the top degree), you must do so now before you extend the offer. Lying is just too common: News reports provide ample examples. For example, Radio Shack's CEO resigned after reporters discovered he lied on his résumé about having degrees in theology and psychology. Bausch and Lomb's CEO and Veritas' CFO also had to resign after their false claims of degrees were discovered (Gross, 2002). InfoLink Screening Services, a background checking company, estimates that 14% of U.S. job applicants lie about their degrees on their résumés (Cullen, 2006). Clearly, lies about credentials are not unique to the executive suite, and the ivory towers are not exempt. You can usually verify degrees by calling a school's records office. Some schools employ a company to handle these requests for them and will provide you with this information when you call.

Some institutions have policies dictating that criminal background and/or credit checks be completed before an offer is finalized. If your institution does not have such a policy, the committee will need to decide what is appropriate. (Some schools conduct checks on all finalists before they are invited to campus so the hiring decision is not delayed, but others wait believing this is an unnecessary expense and invasion of the candidates' privacy.) Several high-profile cases have prompted colleges to reexamine their policies (Smallwood, 2004), and more institutions are now requiring these checks (Vinik, 2005). Colleges are concerned about making good hiring decisions, but they also require checks to avert charges of negligent hiring if problems arise. In *The Complete Reference Checking Handbook,* Andler (2003) notes that an employer can be held liable "when the employer does not reasonably investigate a potential employee's background and puts the employee in a position to commit crimes or exposes others to the risk of harm or injury from that employee" (p. 51).

We want to point out that not all agree that criminal background checks should be routinely required. The American Association of

University Professors (2004) is opposed, arguing the practice should be "limited to candidacies for positions with significant security considerations." The organization argues that the practice compromises the privacy of candidates and is "notoriously imprecise." Certainly background checks are not fail-safe, and all should realize the information obtained is limited.

If you recommend a background check, have a trained HR representative or a professional company conduct it after obtaining the candidate's permission. Specific laws apply, and it is best to work with someone familiar with the laws. (For a synthesis of the law, see Howie & Shapero, 2002.)

## Extend the Offer

When extending the offer, assume candidates have choices and strive to be persuasive. Explain to the candidate why he or she was selected, highlighting strengths, and why your institution is a good fit for him or her. Then give the candidate a reasonable amount of time, such as two weeks, for a response.

If you have any say in the salary offered, we urge you to pay people as well as you can. Let's assume a hiring authority decides a candidate is desperate, and thus they can offer $3,000 less than was offered to another hire at the same level. Such a decision inevitably hurts morale in the long run. The new hire will learn what others are making, and the hiring authority has created ill will and now has a disgruntled employee.

## Tie Up Loose Ends

You have many details to dispense with before the search is finished. For example, you need to:

- Notify candidates not selected as soon as possible. Be honest but don't compare them to the candidate selected.
- Write needed thank-you letters.
- Complete EEO/AA forms and any paperwork required by your HR office.
- Complete files for your unit, keeping copies of needed documents and shredding others. Check with your HR office about what must be kept and for how long. Erase or destroy the phone interview tapes you said would be erased after the search.

- Evaluate the process. What did you do well that others should do in future searches? What could have been done to make the process more efficient? If you did not attract the number of qualified applicants you wanted, particularly from minority groups, what could you and others do differently? Keep a good record of effective and ineffective practices and share this information so others can learn from past experience.

## WELCOME THE NEW HIRE TO CAMPUS

Do what you can to make your new colleague's arrival on campus easy. We have heard stories of new employees arriving on campus to discover their office computer hadn't been ordered or worse—they hadn't been assigned an office. Other new employees tell stories of arriving to a newly painted office, equipped with computer and needed supplies. Taking care of this kind of physical detail helps make a colleague feel welcomed and valued.

Welcoming new hires also includes consideration for their socialization. Walking them around campus and introducing them to others they will interact with is one way to ease their transition. Having a social welcoming gathering is another way. Small things, like asking the new hire to lunch, do matter.

The main way to help new hires is by having unit and institutional practices that support them and let them know they are valued, practices such as mentoring of new faculty and staff, fair evaluation procedures, and faculty and staff development programs. A campus culture that values and supports employees is the best way to welcome and retain good hires.

## CONCLUSION

After reading this book, we hope you see that hiring right isn't a matter of chance or luck. The well-founded strategies and guidelines covered in these pages significantly increase your chances of hiring the right person for your job. By understanding the charge, establishing clear operating procedures, and learning the legalities, the search committee starts out on solid ground. Taking time to analyze the position carefully and write a compelling position announcement helps ensure an effective, legal, and defensible process. Adopting the suggestions for recruiting diverse and highly qualified applicants contributes to a strong pool of candidates. Once candidate materials are submitted, following the steps of reviewing files, identifying top candidates, and carefully gathering and evaluating information results in valid and defensible decisions about which candidates to bring to campus. Careful planning and effective communication with all involved improve the quality of the campus visit. Searches are not ever likely to be easy, but they can be effective and less painful by understanding and following best practices and communicating effectively throughout the process. Your success in hiring right will contribute to the ongoing excellence of your unit and institution.

# Appendix A

## Sample Tracking Forms

### TRACKING FORM FOR APPLICATION COMPLETENESS AND CORRESPONDENCE

| Candidate Name | Cover Letter | Vita | Application Form | Unofficial Transcripts | Statement of Philosophy | Reference Letter #1 | Reference Letter #2 | Reference Letter #3 | Letter of Receipt Sent |
|---|---|---|---|---|---|---|---|---|---|
| Candidate #1 | | | | | | | | | |
| Candidate #2 | | | | | | | | | |
| Candidate #3 | | | | | | | | | |
| Candidate #4 | | | | | | | | | |
| | | | | | | | | | |
| | | | | | | | | | |
| | | | | | | | | | |

# CHECKLIST FOR COMPLETENESS OF EACH FILE

**Received from Candidate**

_____ Cover letter/letter of application

_____ Vita

_____ Application form

_____ Transcripts (unofficial, all degree-granting institutions)

_____ Statement of philosophy

_____ Reference letters

    1. _____ Email for reference: _____

    2. _____ Email for reference: _____

    3. _____ Email for reference: _____

**Sent to Candidate**

_____ Letter acknowledging receipt of application

_____ Letter closing applicant's search file

# Appendix B

# Sample Letters

**Letter to Acknowledge Receipt of Application**

See Chapter 4 for sample.

**Rejection Letter to Candidates in the *No* Group**

Dear _____:

The search committee for the position of _____ has narrowed the applicant pool to a small group of candidates whose credentials best suit our needs. I regret to inform you that you are not in this pool. You should know that our deliberations were difficult because we had a number of excellent applicants.

I thank you for your interest in [name of university] and wish you success in your career search.

Sincerely,

Search Committee Chair

**Rejection Letter to Semi-Finalists**

Dear _____:

The search committee for the position of _____ has now completed the phone interviews and selected a small number of candidates to invite to campus. I regret to inform you that you are not in this group. The committee's deliberations were quite difficult because we had several excellent candidates.

Thank you for your interest in [name of university] and for taking the time to participate in the phone interview. I wish you success in your job search.

Sincerely,

Search Committee Chair

## Letter for Candidates on the Reserve List

Dear _____:

The search committee for the position of _____ has completed its review of candidate files. We were fortunate to have several well-qualified applicants, and we have selected a small group of candidates whose credentials best match our needs to move forward to the next step in the selection process. Although we are sorry to say that you are not in this group, committee members were impressed with your credentials and would like to keep your application on file and in a reserve pool. We will return to this pool if needed.

I will notify you if your status changes or when we complete the search. Thank you for your interest in [name of university].

Sincerely,

Search Committee Chair

## Rejection Letter to Finalists

Dear _____:

The search committee for the position of _____ has now completed its deliberations and selected a candidate who has accepted our offer. You should know we had a difficult task because we had outstanding finalists and unfortunately could select only one person.

We appreciate your visiting our campus, and we enjoyed meeting you. [If possible, personalize this letter by adding a positive statement here about a candidate's campus visit. For example, you could thank a candidate for speaking to a student group and tell him or her that the students learned much from the presentation. One positive statement is sufficient—don't go overboard.]

We wish you success in your career.

Sincerely,

Search Committee Chair

# Appendix C

## Sample Email to Semi-Finalists

Dear _____:

I am writing to you in my capacity as chair of the _____ Search Committee. On behalf of the committee, I am pleased to inform you that we would like to interview you over the phone and, with your permission, begin to check references for you. Below I have listed some times I am available for a phone interview and ask that you look these over and, if at all possible, list two of the times you are available. (If you have a preference, also give this.) If the times below do not suit your schedule, let me know and send at least four different times you are available. Please note that we are on Eastern Standard Time.

[List days and times of availability]

Because not all committee members are able to be present for the phone interviews, we would like to tape these interviews, and I ask for your permission to do this. We would like for all members to have the opportunity to hear all interviews. After the search, the tape will be erased or destroyed. When you reply to this message, please let me know if this is acceptable.

In addition, we will soon begin the process of contacting references. To do so, we would like you to send us the email addresses of your references. We also ask for permission to contact unlisted references. If there is anyone we should not contact at this time, please let us know.

In your reply, we need the following information:

- Times you are available
- The best number for reaching you

- Permission to tape the interview
- Email addresses for your listed references
- Permission to contact unlisted references (If yes, is there anyone we should not contact?)

We are pleased that you are interested in the position of _____ at our institution and we look forward to talking with you. I will contact you as soon as possible with a specific interview time.

Sincerely,

Search Committee Chair

# Bibliography

ABC News. (2006, February 21). Edmondson not only one lying on resume. Retrieved May 30, 2007, from http://abcnews.go.com/GMA/print?id=1643683

Adler, R. B., Rosenfeld, L. B., & Proctor, R. F., II. (2007). *Interplay: The process of interpersonal communication* (10th ed.). New York, NY: Oxford University Press.

American Association of University Professors. (2004, April 24). *AAUP comments on faculty background checks* [Press release]. Retrieved May 30, 2007, from www.aaup.org/AAUP/newsroom/prarchives/2004/back.htm?PF=1

Andler, E. C. (2003). *The complete reference checking handbook: The proven (and legal) way to prevent hiring mistakes* (2nd ed.). New York, NY: AMACOM.

Arvey, R. D., & Campion, J. E. (1982, Summer). The employment interview: A summary and review of recent research. *Personnel Psychology, 35*(2), 281–322.

Basinger, J. (2004, March 5). Four years after a scandal, a president steps down. *The Chronicle of Higher Education,* pp. A23–A24.

Bernard, P. J. (2006, September 29). When seeking a diverse faculty, watch out for legal minefields. *The Chronicle of Higher Education,* pp. B28–B31.

Bolles, R. N. (2001). *What color is your parachute? A practical manual for job-hunters and career-changers.* Berkeley, CA: Ten Speed Press.

Broome, B. J. (2000). Palevome: Foundations of struggle and conflict in Greek interpersonal communication. In L. A. Samovar & R. E. Porter (Eds.), *Intercultural communication: A reader* (9th ed., pp. 105–114). Belmont, CA: Wadsworth.

Campion, M. A., Palmer, D. K., & Campion, J. E. (1997, Autumn). A review of structure in the selection interview. *Personnel Psychology, 50*(3), 655–702.

Collins, J. (2001). *Good to great: Why some companies make the leap . . . and others don't.* New York, NY: HarperCollins.

Cullen, L. T. (2006, May 1). Getting wise to lies. *Time, 167*(18), 59.

Dettmar, K. J. H. (2004, December 17). What we waste when faculty hiring goes wrong. *The Chronicle of Higher Education,* p. B6.

ESPN.com. (2001, December 14). Academic, athletic irregularities force resignation. Retrieved May 30, 2007, from http://espn.go.com/ncf/news/2001/1214/1295624.html

Fogg, P. (2006, September 19). Panel blames bias for gender gap. *The Chronicle of Higher Education,* p. A13.

Fonda, D., & Healy, R. (2005, September 8). How reliable is Brown's resume? *Time* [Online ed.]. Retrieved May 30, 2007, from www.time.com/time/nation/article/0,8599,1103003,00.html

Gerken, H. K. (1993, June). Understanding mixed motives claims under the Civil Rights Act of 1991: An analysis of intentional discrimination claims based on sex-stereotyped interview questions. *Michigan Law Review, 91*(7), 1824–1853.

Gilliland, S. W., & Steiner, D. D. (1999). Applicant reactions. In R. W. Eder & M. M. Harris (Eds.), *The employment interview handbook* (2nd ed., pp. 69–82). Thousand Oaks, CA: Sage.

Gross, D. (2002). *School lies: Why do so many executives lie about their education?* Retrieved May 30, 2007, from www.slate.com/id/2072961/

Hall, B. (2005). *Among cultures: The challenge of communication* (2nd ed.). Belmont, CA: Wadsworth.

Herriott, P. (2003, June). Assessment by groups: Can value be added? *European Journal of Work and Organizational Psychology, 12*(2), 131–145.

HireSmart. (2006). *How to avoid costly hiring mistakes.* Retrieved May 29, 2007, from www.hiresmart.com/marketing/avoid/index.stm

Howie, R. M., & Shapero, L. A. (2002, Summer). Pre-employment criminal background checks: Why employers should look before they leap. *Employee Relations Law Journal, 28*(1), 63–77.

Huffcutt, A. I., & Arthur, W. (1994, April). Hunter and Hunter (1984) revisited: Interview validity for entry-level jobs. *Journal of Applied Psychology, 79*(2), 184–190.

Hussar, W. J., & Bailey, T. M. (2006, September). *Projections of education statistics to 2015* (NCES Publication No. 2006–084). U.S. Department of Education, National Center for Education Statistics. Washington, DC: U.S. Government Printing Office.

Ilkka, R. J. (1995, September). Applicant appearance and selection decision making: Revitalizing employment interview education. *Business Communication Quarterly, 58*(3), 11–18.

Kellerman, K. (1989, Winter). The negativity effect in interaction: It's all in your point of view. *Human Communication Research, 16*(2), 147–183.

Kellough, J. E. (2006). *Understanding affirmative action: Politics, discrimination, and the search for justice.* Washington, DC: Georgetown University Press.

Kirkwood, W. G., & Ralston, S. M. (1999, January). Inviting meaningful applicant performances in employment interviews. *Journal of Business Communication, 36*(1), 55–76.

Kluger, J. (2002, June 10). Pumping up your past. *Time, 159*(23), 45.

Knapp, L. G., Kelly-Reid, J. E., Whitmore, R. W., Huh, S., Zhao, L., Levine, B., et al. (2005). *Staff in postsecondary institutions, fall 2003, and salaries of full-time instructional faculty, 2003–04* (NCES Publication No. 2005–155). U.S. Department of Education. Washington, DC: National Center for Education Statistics.

Knapp, M. L., & Hall, J. A. (2002). *Nonverbal communication in human interaction* (5th ed.). Belmont, CA: Wadsworth.

Knapp, M. L., & Hall, J. A. (2006). *Nonverbal communication in human interaction* (6th ed.). Belmont, CA: Wadsworth.

Marlowe, C. M., Schneider, S. L., & Nelson, C. E. (1996, February). Gender and attractiveness bias in hiring decisions: Are more experienced managers less biased? *Journal of Applied Psychology, 81*(1), 11–21.

McDaniel, M. A., Whetzel, D. L., Schmidt, F. L., & Maurer, S. D. (1994, August). The validity of employment interviews: A comprehensive review and meta-analysis. *Journal of Applied Psychology, 79*(4), 599–616.

Nelson, G., & Olwell, R. (2002, Summer). Using teaching portfolios in faculty job searches: One department's recent experiences. *The Department Chair, 13*(1), 22, 24.

Ralston, S. M., & Brady, R. (1994, January). The relative influence of interview communication satisfaction on applicants' recruitment interview decisions. *Journal of Business Communication, 31*(1), 61–77.

Roehling, M. V. (1999, December). Weight-based discrimination in employment: Psychological and legal aspects. *Personnel Psychology, 52*(4), 969–1016.

Rothwell, J. D. (2004). *In mixed company: Communicating in small groups and teams* (5th ed.). Belmont, CA: Wadsworth.

Salgado, J. F., & Moscoso, S. (2002, September). Comprehensive meta-analysis of the construct validity of the employment interview. *European Journal of Work and Organizational Psychology, 11*(3), 299–324.

Schmidt, F. L., & Hunter, J. E. (1998, September). The validity and utility of selection methods in personnel psychology: Practical and theoretical implications of 85 years of research findings. *Psychological Bulletin, 124*(2), 262–274.

Semic, B. (1999). Vocal attractiveness: What sounds beautiful is good. In L. K. Guerrero, J. A. DeVito, & M. L. Hecht (Eds.), *The nonverbal communication reader: Classic and contemporary readings* (2nd ed., pp. 149–155). Prospect Heights, IL: Waveland Press.

Smallwood, S. (2004, July 30). No surprises, please. *The Chronicle of Higher Education*, p. A8.

Smith, D. (2000, September–October). How to diversify the faculty. *Academe*, *86*(5), 48–52.

Smith, D. G., & Moreno, J. F. (2006, September 29). Hiring the next generation of professors: Will myths remain excuses? *The Chronicle of Higher Education*, pp. B22–B24.

Stokes, P. P. (2000, Summer/Fall). Is there a duty to disclose in employment references? (Honesty is the best policy). *Business Forum, 25*(3/4), 11–16.

Ting-Toomey, S., & Chung, L. C. (2005). *Understanding intercultural communication*. Los Angeles, CA: Roxbury.

Trower, C. A., & Chait, R. P. (2002, March/April). Faculty diversity: Too little for too long. *Harvard Magazine, 104*(4), 33–38.

Turner, C. S. V. (2002). *Diversifying the faculty: A guidebook for search committees*. Washington, DC: Association of American Colleges and Universities.

Umbach, P. D., & Kuh, G. D. (2006, January/February). Student experiences with diversity at liberal arts colleges: Another claim for distinctiveness. *Journal of Higher Education, 77*(1), 169–192.

Vinik, D. F. (2005, May 27). Why background checks matter in academe. *The Chronicle of Higher Education*, p. B31.

Weiss, D. H. (2004). *Fair, square and legal: Safe hiring, managing and firing practices to keep you and your company out of court* (4th ed.). New York, NY: AMACOM.

Wilson, R. (2003, November 28). Wanted: Hispanic professors. *The Chronicle of Higher Education*, p. A15.

# Index

AAUP, *see* American Association of University
    Professors
ABC News, 47, 107
Accents, 92
Accreditation, 47–48, 72
Ad/advertising, *see* Diversity; Position
    announcement; Recruitment
Adler, R., 54, 107
Affirmative Action, 17, 27, 109
*Affirmative Action Registry, The*, 35
Age Discrimination Act, 13
Alumni, 8–9, 34, 50, 83, 84
American Association of University
    Professors, 96–97, 107
Americans with Disabilities Act, 13, 59
Andler, E., 67, 96, 107
Applicant, *see* Candidates
Applications, *see* Files, candidate
Arrest record, 16
Arthur, W., 79, 107
Arvey, R., 78, 107
Audiotaping, 56, 64–66, 71

Background checks, 96–97, 107, 108, 110
Bailey, T. M., 33, 108
Basinger, J., 44, 107
Bernard, P., 17, 107
BFOQs, 13, 16, 58–59, 71, 90–92
Biases, 91–92
Bolles, R. N., 77, 107
Bona fide occupational qualifications, *see*
    BFOQs
Brady, R., 87, 109
Broome, B., 53, 107
Brown, Michael, 46, 108

Campion, J., 61, 78–79, 86, 107
Campion, M., 61, 78–79, 86, 107
Campus visit, 11, 68, 74–75, 77–88, 92–93
    getting feedback, 80–82, 84–85
    interviews during, 4, 22, 77–80, 83–87
    involving others, 83–85

itinerary, 85–87
    preparing participants, 86
    *see also* Information gathering methods;
        Interviews
Candidates
    communication with, *see* Communication,
        with applicants
    internal, 12, 59, 68
    unqualified, 11, 23, 40, 45
    wooing, 86–88
Chait, R. P., 33, 110
*Chronicle of Higher Education, The*, 3, 17, 23,
    25–27, 30, 32, 41, 107–108, 110
Chung, L., 53, 110
Civil Rights Act, 13
Claremont Graduate University, 34–35
Collins, Jim, 1, 108
Committee, *see* Search committee
Communication
    as recruitment tool, 31–34
    of next step, 64, 74–75, 88, 104
    with applicants, 31–34, 55–56, 68, 74–75,
        88, 97, 103–106
    within committee, 12, 65, 74, 90–91, 93–95
Community members, 8, 11, 84
Confidentiality, 10, 12, 90
Consensus, 12
Credit checks, 96
Critique of work, 78, 80
Cullen, L. T., 96, 108
Cultural issues, 4, 9, 28, 52–53
Curriculum vitae/CV, *see* Vitae

Deadlines, 21–23
Decision, defending, 5, 40, 95–96
Decision-making, 39–54, 89–95
    evaluating negative information, 45, 48–54,
        73–74, 90
    procedures for, 10–12, 55, 74, 90, 93–94
    *yes, no, maybe* groups, 12, 40–43, 55, 74
    *see also* Deliberations, final
Degrees, 20, 72, 102